MW01487889

The Gathering of Eagles

A Prophetic Word to America and the Church

To my Brother Mike,
May God Bless everything you loved.
God Bless you!

By

PASTOR LARRY BISHOP

Dove Ministries
www.DoveMinistry.org
918-296-0077

Pastor Larry Bishop

11/28/17

COPYRIGHT

Copyright ©2016 The Gathering of Eagles: by Pastor Larry Bishop

ISBN-13: 978-1547255269

ISBN-10: 1547255269

Unless otherwise noted, all scriptures taken from the King James Version of the Bible. New King James Version (NKJV) The Holy Bible, New King James Version Copyright © 1982 by Thomas Nelson,Inc.

DEDICATION

I dedicate this book to my wife, Linda of forty-nine years, and to my children, Becky and Jason, who have been faithful throughout the years for the Gospel's sake.

BIOGRAPHY

Pastor Larry G. Bishop is the founder and senior pastor of Dove Ministry in Jenks, OK. Pastor Larry is known for his love, integrity, and sensitivity to the Holy Spirit. Prior to accepting God's mandate to pastor, he and his wife, Linda, were successful business owners starting many successful companies. Out of obedience to the Holy Spirit, they surrendered it all to become full-time evangelists, where they traveled the United States for over twenty years. Throughout their ministry, they have brought healing and restoration to the body of Christ through the anointing of the Holy Spirit. He has been pastoring for over eighteen years. Their ministry continues to see miracles, signs, and wonders as they function in divine gifts.

TABLE OF CONTENTS

The Gathering of Eagles

A MESSAGE
FROM PASTOR LARRY BISHOP

ISAIAH 40:31

"But they that wait upon the Lord shall renew their strength; they shall mount up with wings as eagles; they shall run, and not be weary; and they shall walk, and not faint."

I am excited about this word. I pray as you read you will be blessed. We have heard many prophecies about the gathering of the eagles. As I study the Word I have discovered something profound and timely. This book is to show you what I believe the Lord has

7

revealed to me and some of the historic times we are living in. I believe this is a word for right now. There have been many people who are knowledgeable about the Word of God. There are many that might really know the Word, but get discouraged because they don't understand how to use it in their lives for a victory. I believe, like the sons of Issachar, we are given the revelation to understand the times we are living in.

I have learned over the years it is not the intensity of the spoken word that you need to understand, but it is the **clarity of thought** you grasp in order to understand.

There is a gathering of the eagles (believers) taking place where divisions will no longer be a problem, but we are coming into a great unity for the purpose and plans of God. This book alone is a prophetic fulfillment of the Holy Spirit in my life to speak to the hearts of the eagles He is gathering. We have people coming from all over the United States and the World so full of the Holy Spirit and they want to find a place where they can gather together and enjoy the presence of the Lord. It won't be church as usual. It will be a place that is prepared, sanctified, and set apart that is holy for God.

It will be a place that will be a portal where God has written His name, "Jehovah is here." It will be a place that people will say is like a little piece of Heaven, a Jerusalem, and they have found it. God is wanting His people to gather, but there are reasons we don't see this gathering in churches right now. There are reasons such as, people are hurting! I believe that after you read this book you will have a purpose and a plan in life that you have never thought of before. I have been a minister of the gospel for over forty years and I have read this scripture, Isaiah 40:31 many times. I have thought and prayed about it, but I believe now the revelation will enlighten you to the place where you will want to do something. I have learned over the years it is not the intensity of the spoken word that you need to understand, but it is the **clarity of thought** you grasp in order to understand. It is one of the reasons I decided to write this book. Words when written down have a specific clarity and revelation. Through reading this book you will want to place yourself in the middle of what God is doing. You are not just reading this book by accident or happenstance. You are the blessed seed of Abraham and this Word is for you.

INTRODUCTION

Jesus had a very unique way of communicating with people. He was known for His incredible ability to tell a parable and to explain important points. He wanted people to understand how His Father wanted them to live in order to have a good, prosperous, and healthy life. A parable is a short illustration or story that makes the impact of His purpose seen easily and clearly. He wanted the hearer to understand and to put into practice what they learned from the parable.

This book is a story or a parable that the Holy Spirit put on my heart to reach hurting people. As a pastor, I meet people all the time who are going through incredible sorrow, pain, and disillusionment. They are experiencing dire circumstances and really just want to quit life. As a pastor, compassion flows out of me and I want to help them realize that Jesus loves them and things will get better. This story I am about to tell you should encourage you, give you hope, and teach you of your Savior's divine plan for your life and your purpose.

This book is a profound parable about eagles and it is meant to be instructive to the reader. It will be a simple narrative and will describe a very peculiar action that great eagles go through. It will illustrate the moral and crisis situations we often find our lives falling into. This story is not meant to be difficult to understand, but I have tried to be straightforward and self-explanatory. It will provide guidance and encouragement to the hurting.

Let me give you an example of a parable story. It is called *The Rooster Prince* or *The Turkey Prince*. It is a Jewish story and was told by Rabbi Nachman of Breslov, a founder of Hasidic Judaism.

"In this story, a prince goes insane and believes that he is a rooster (or turkey). He takes off his clothes, sits naked under the table, and pecks at his food on the floor. The king and queen are horrified that the heir to the throne is acting this way. They call in various sages and healers to try and convince the prince to act human again, but to no avail. Then a new wise man comes to the palace and claims he can cure the prince. He takes off his clothes and sits naked under the table with him, claiming to be a rooster, too. Gradually, the prince comes to accept him as a friend. The sage then tells the prince that a rooster can wear clothes, eat at the table, etc. The Rooster Prince accepts this idea and, step-by-step, begins to act normally, until he is completely cured."

The main interpretation of this story is that the prince represents a simple Jew who has forgotten his true self, and the sage represents a wise man who has the cure for his soul. Rather than condemn the simple one he descends to his level to meet him where he is, then show him how to return to God, step-by-step, and in a manner they can accept.

This story is simple, but shows the main point of when you lose focus of who you really are, in Christ, usually it takes a pastor or someone in what is known as the five-fold ministry to help you back to that unconditional love that Jesus offers you. (http://www.breslov.org)

This story that I am about to tell you is a parable based on a real life story. It is about eagles and what actually happens in their life span. It is simple and it is a tremendous example to show you how the hurting can be restored, and live to soar again. This story is about the molting of the eagles.

Chapter 1

ARE YOU SEEING AND HEARING?

As a pastor, I would say that a great deal of my time is spent dealing with questions and answers. People want to know things, people want to understand, but unfortunately many never come to the knowledge or understanding of their answers even though they hear the answer clearly. Why?

Matthew 13: 9, 10, 11, *"Whoever hath ears to hear, let him hear. And the disciples came, and said unto him, Why speakest thou unto them in parables? He answered and said unto them, because it is given unto you to know the mysteries of the kingdom of heaven, but to them it is not given."*

15

Matthew 13: 13, *"Therefore speak I to them in parables: because they seeing see not; and hearing they hear not, neither do they understand. And in them is fulfilled the prophecy of Esaias, which saith, by hearing ye shall hear, and shall not understand;"*

If you know Scripture you know that the disciples of Jesus had questions to ask Him. Have you ever had questions? I encourage you to ask the Holy Spirit questions to teach you. The disciples asked Jesus why He spoke in parables. Parables actually stir us. Most preachers will usually preach in a parable that will help you to understand how the Word of God applies to you, and where you are at the current time. Jesus explained things in parables and comparisons in many different ways. I want to get the Word of God applied to you because it is like a salve applied to the wounds and hurts of yesterday and today. You have to have an understanding of how it applies to you, and what you should do. When you don't know, just do what Jesus did.

Jesus is the head of the Kingdom of Heaven. People who are not interested in understanding these mysteries will not be able to understand the parables. It is important as you read this book to tell yourself, "Get interested." This is the day to get interested. As I questioned the Lord about this study I asked, "Lord are people really this disinterested?"

The Lord answered me, "My people are going to be awakened to what I am going to do."

As I studied this topic I was reminded of Daniel chapter two, where God says He raises up kings and brings down kings. We have just had a major election in America. His hand was upon this election and now we will see how God will use it to gather the eagles. So watch and pray!

One of the main problems in the Church today is complacency and being lukewarm. God said, "I would rather you be hot or cold."

We are going to have revelation that no one else has. May the Word of God have free course in our nation and may God bless new leadership with a revelation of who He is and what He wants to do.

May the Holy Spirit teach you revelation!

2 Thessalonians 3:1, *"Finally, brethren, pray for us, that the word of the Lord may have free course, and be glorified, even as it is with you."*

MATTHEW 13: 12

"For whosoever hath, to him shall be given, and he shall have more abundance: but whosoever hath not, from him shall be taken away even that he hath."

One of the main problems in the Church today is complacency and being lukewarm. God said, "I would rather you be hot or cold. I would rather you be for me or against me, but don't be lukewarm! Just love me." God is going to shake you to the roots if you get lukewarm. I'm praying that you get on fire for God!

You are not too old. As long as you are breathing you are subject to a mystery. Sometimes you get to the place where you think God can't use you. Today, I am shaking you up to tell you that you can't be lukewarm anymore. If you are lukewarm He spews you out of His mouth. I'm trying to wake you up and put you back into a place of fire!

Christians have come to the place where they will swallow any false doctrine. They'll believe almost anything. Do you ever feel like when you are talking to somebody that you are talking to a wall? You have to wake up and ask the Holy Spirit to give you understanding of our times. The sons of Issachar knew the times and the seasons they were living in. 1Chronicles 12:32 says, *"And the children of Issachar, which were men that had understanding of the times, to know what Israel ought to do; the heads of them were two hundred; and all their brethren were at their commandment."*

Many scholars believe these were politically aware men who were able to understand the time for David to take the throne of Israel. We have to understand what time it is, so we can accomplish what God wants to do. As we come together in unity with new and very different leadership we should be able to discern the times we will be living in. So put your hand on your heart and say, "Lord I repent of being lukewarm. I haven't been listening to my Holy Ghost clock. I need to pay attention. From this day forward I want to understand the mysteries of God."

God will show us the prophetic purpose for our seasons of life if we will pray, study, and allow the Holy Spirit to speak to us. He is wanting to show us the mysteries.

MATTHEW 13: 14, 15

"And in them is fulfilled the prophecy of Esaias, which saith, By hearing ye shall hear, and shall not understand; and seeing ye shall see, and shall not perceive: For this people's heart is waxed gross, and their ears are dull of hearing, and their eyes they have closed; lest at any time they should see with their eyes and hear with their ears, and should understand with their heart, and should be converted, and I should heal them."

This fulfills the prophecy of Isaiah. When people become dull of hearing you might as well be talking to a fence post. Let me tell you about a lady that I met in New Orleans, during a revival meeting. This lady got saved, and I didn't know until after she got saved that she had been a witch, before her conversion. God loves us all and He can save anybody. Before her salvation she was putting hexes on people in the church. Sometimes, there are witches and warlocks assigned to churches. I saw a lot of it in New

Orleans. We have been so educated that we do not understand how severe this can be to try and neutralize us from our abilities to do something for God. I sat down with her because I had a lot of questions. I asked, "Why did you give your heart to the Lord, I'm just curious; especially after serving Satan like you did?"

I asked her who her choice was and she told me Jesus Christ because He is the only One who has truth and true power. He is the only One who paid the price for her to be redeemed.

She said, "Well, I've tried everything Satan had and he didn't have anything, but there was an enjoyment of power that Satan gave me to hex people. I saw clearly how these hexes destroyed everything that God was giving and I began to think, "Why do I have to destroy everything that God loves? I became convicted by the Holy Spirit, because of the preaching of the gospel. It was made so plain through illustration of what you were doing that I had no choice, but to choose who I was going to serve."

I asked her who her choice was and she told me Jesus Christ, because He is the only One who has truth and true power. He is the only One who paid the price for her to be redeemed. "When I confessed Him out of my mouth I received something from Him that I never received from Satan.

Romans 10: 9, 10,

"That if thou shalt confess with thy mouth the Lord Jesus, and shalt believe in thine heart that God hath raised him from the dead, thou shalt be saved. For with the heart man believeth unto righteousness; and with the mouth confession is made unto salvation."

"All I received from Satan was a demand to put more curses on people for his glory. All I received from Jesus was more light and understanding of who I was. I could be a better person to bring life, instead of death, through understanding who Jesus is. So I decided to be a minister of life from that day forward."

She asked me if she could share something with me and I responded that she could, because that is the reason I was talking to her. She said,

22

"Wherever you go in your ministry tell people that at some point in their life they may have had an encounter with someone who loved demonic power. Tell them that this false power attacks the inner ear first."

I asked, "Why is that?"

She replied, "Faith comes by hearing and hearing by the Word of God. In the spirit realm wherever the blood of Jesus has been applied to the inner ear the devil cannot attack the Word. So tell the people to cover their ears with the redeemed blood of Jesus Christ, and your ears will never stop hearing and understanding the mysteries of the Kingdom of God. People become so dull of hearing and can't understand that somebody spoke over them a curse and a demonic power came into their inner ear, but in Christ, we have the authority to break it so that we can be blessed in everything we do.

As I get to the parable of *The Gathering of Eagles* in the next chapters I want you to be able to hear, see, and understand this mystery; so that the love of Jesus can reach you in a unique and powerful way. Pray over your ears right now:

"Lord Jesus by the power of the blood of Jesus I know that faith comes by hearing and hearing by the Word of God. I break the curse of not being able to hear. My faith is going to be greater than it ever has been since I began worshiping the Lord Jesus Christ. The mysteries of the Scriptures will not be hidden from me anymore, because the blood has cleansed the avenue for me to have faith in Jesus, and has already agreed with the Father, Son, and the Holy Ghost. Now Holy Ghost you have permission to come and teach me the truth and understanding of the mysteries of God. From this day forth I will not be hindered by anything. The truth will set me free in Jesus name." Amen.

Romans 10:17, "So then faith cometh by hearing and hearing by the word of God."

She continued, "What people don't realize is that there is a devil, and the devil wants you to deny that there is even a hell. Hell is real and hell is hot! When you get into a covenant with Satan he does not care if he kills you. He just wants to use you up and destroy you because he came to kill, steal, and destroy you." She knew the Word, but she said, "Until I made up my mind that I was going to quit cursing the ears of people He didn't open mine to the mysteries of Heaven. It came through confession of Jesus name. When you confess Jesus, repent, and ask for the ability to understand the things of God, you are not the same anymore. Now the Holy Spirit can speak the Word to you and you can rejoice because it

> The Damascus road experience was to remove the scales that were put on Saul's (Paul's) eyes because he refused to see what God was doing.

has been given to you the ability to hear what the Spirit is saying and enjoy knowing the mysteries of the Kingdom of God."

Sometimes we close our eyes to the things of God. The Damascus road experience was to remove the scales that were put on Saul's (Paul's) eyes because he refused to see what God was doing. Paul had a zeal to persecute believers. When he was knocked off his horse he stood up blind. Saul did not become Paul until he came through that blind experience. He came out with full hearing and full vision.

So I would like for you to get enlightened in your eyes. You hear the Word, you retain the Word, and faith comes. Now when you get the scales off your eyes you are going to be able to read the Word and the Word will become alive. The Holy Spirit will teach you through the cleansing of the ears. You will have a faith like you have never had before. When you read this time you will say, "I never saw that before, or when did they put that in there?"

It will become alive to you. It will become a time where you will just know where to go and what to do. The Holy Spirit knows what you have need of in the Word of God before you even ask. Pray this, "I ask you Holy Spirit to open my eyes the same way you opened my ears. Apply the blood over my eyes so that I can see spiritually."

Ananias came and prayed for Saul who became Paul. Saul was blind, but after he had his Damascus road experience he heard, saw, and wrote two thirds of the New Testament. Put your hands over your eyes, and repeat this prayer, "Father in the name of Jesus remove the scales that are hindering the Word of God to have free course in my life. I want to hear, and understand.

I give you permission to open my eyes and let me see the mysteries for this time and season. Holy Spirit you have permission by the power of the blood of the Lord Jesus Christ, that the plank in my eye will be removed. I will quit questioning what the Word says, and live by the Word as it is written. I can have full understanding, full revelation, and the Urim and Thummim of God's Word will come to me. I will have understanding upon everything I read and hear, and my soul will be blessed. I will be healed and restored. Everything I touch will be blessed and no weapon formed against me will ever prosper from this day forward, ever again, by the power of the Father, Son, and Holy Ghost in the name of Jesus." Amen.

Let's take a quick look at what I mean about the Urim and Thurmmim. The Urim means *complete light* and the Thurmmim means *complete truth*. They were probably precious stones that the priesthood used to get direct answers from God. They were to be put in the breastplate and in a pocket over Aaron's heart when he stood before the Lord to minister to Him. They were a means used to get any answer, to any problem, which concerned Israel. In a way, I am asking the Holy Spirit to bring to your spiritual eyesight the pure Light and Truth of God's Word so that you can see the clear, pure, and complete picture of what God is revealing to you. Now, praise God you don't need a 'seeing eye' dog anymore. The Word of God cannot have free course in your life until you are delivered of anything unreasonable and wicked. With the illumination of the Holy Spirit He will direct you in a righteous path and life.

Matthew 13:16, *"But blessed are your eyes, for they see: and your ears, for they hear."*

How can you have blessed eyes and ears if they are plugged up?

2 THESSALONIANS 3: 1-3 PAUL'S PRAYER

"Finally, brethren, pray for us, that the word of the Lord may have free course, and be glorified, even as it is with you: And that we may be delivered from unreasonable and wicked men: for all men have not faith. But the Lord is faithful, who shall stablish you, and keep you from evil."

How can the Word of God have free course if you are deaf and blind? You have no excuse if you believe in the death and resurrection of Jesus

Christ! When something has free course it has the right to root out the stupidity and replace it with the Truth. When the Word of God has free course it will lead you in the path of righteousness. Look at the Mississippi River it doesn't ask permission to flow. It will go where it wants and wash out what's in front of it.

> If you can hear, see, and you are letting the Word of God have free course, it does not matter your age. God gives us power, love, and a sound mind. You can have everything God has for you.

When something has free course in your life, whatever has been hindering you, the Word will wash it away and give you another avenue to worship in freedom and truth.

How many of you want a new avenue to worship? Have you ever asked yourself why one person is so excited about the gospel, but you are not? Is it because you are blind and deaf? The Word of God has not been able to have free course in your life. The airways are full of preaching. Why haven't you heard? There's too much static, too many things to look at and hear, besides the gospel. If you prayed the prayers I gave you for the opening of your eyes and ears the Holy Spirit will come and live in the habitation of Truth and teach you all things.

How is He going to establish to keep you from evil if you can't see and hear? If you can hear, see, and you are letting the Word of God have free course, it does not matter your age. God gives us power, love, and a sound mind. You can have everything God has for you. I am going to be restored, I am going to be healed, I am going to get the overflow of God, and I expect the performance of the Word, as I preach. I am going to let the Word of God have free course. I have revealed to you the secret of hearing and seeing. This kind of wisdom is not for you to think you are something you are not. This kind of wisdom is from God to bring others out of darkness!

I have written this book so you can understand a powerful parable about *The Gathering of Eagles*.

Matthew 13:18

"Hear ye therefore the parable of the sower."

Chapter 2

THE EAGLE

When you begin to do a basic study of the eagle you find that the species is divided into four groups. The grouping is based on the physical characteristics and certain behaviors. Fish Eagles, like the name implies eat a lot of fish. Snake or Serpent Eagles do the same with snakes. Harpy Eagles strike larger prey. It has been seen through video shots that eagles can snatch monkeys out of trees. They usually don't carry their prey back to their nest, but feast on the carcass for a few days. The last group is the Booted Eagle. These eagles get their name because their feathers grow down to their ankles. This group of eagles are known for their majestic beauty and are some the largest eagles in the world. Today, eagles have become very vulnerable to the changing environments and population growth. So much so that governments around the world have passed laws to try to preserve them from extinction.

Many believers have also been influenced by the culture, environment, and worldly pleasures. This book is an attempt, through the power of the Holy Spirit's wisdom, to preserve the body of Christ.

Jesus in one of His greatest sermons stops in the middle and gives some directions to the people.

Matthew 6:26

"Behold the fowls of the air: for they sow not, neither do they reap, nor gather into barns; yet your heavenly Father feedeth them. Are you not much better than they?"

God wants us to look at the birds and understand that He is using them as an illustration as to show us how He cares for us and feeds us. As I studied eagles I was amazed at the plan of God for our lives that He shows through the lifespan of an eagle. The Bald Eagle is the American symbol. It is our national bird and I believe when you understand the molting process of the eagle you will clearly see where America is at this time in history. It is time to see the prophetic word for our nation through this parable of the molting eagle.

The eagle is majestic, powerful, and incredibly strong. America in its beginnings was the jewel of the world. It became the most powerful nation in the world. We soared as a watchmen for freedom all over the world.

The Church was the foundation for all our documents and even the buildings, money, and history of America. "In God We Trust," is the motto of our nation and it is the central foundational principle of the Church. President Thomas Jefferson said it plainly, "The God who gave us life gave us liberty at the same time. Can the liberties of a nation be secure when we have removed a conviction that these liberties are of God?"

America is forsaking the God who gave us this freedom. Today, the Church is forsaking purity and holiness as its foundation. "In God We Trust" is found repeatedly in the Scriptures.

Psalm 118:8, *"It is better to trust in the LORD than to put confidence in man."*

Proverbs 29:25

"The fear of man brings a snare: but whoso putteth his trust in the LORD shall be safe."

All one has to do is read a newspaper, get on Facebook, or other social media to learn that people are moving away from the gospel of Jesus Christ and America, right now, is a reflection of that loss.

America is now going through natural disasters, social unrest, and terrorism! We are not soaring like the great eagle of freedom any longer because we are not putting our trust in the Lord! The Church finds itself compromised because we are not leading this nation and its people in righteousness at the moment. The *molting* or loss of greatness is everywhere. The government, the medical, the social, the military and crime have gotten to depressing and out of control realms.

People are depressed, scared and empty. We need the blessing of God again in the nation and the Church. *The Gathering of Eagles* is one way God is calling us together to demonstrate His power through the gifts of the Holy Spirit operating in a divine unity of believers.

The name "bald" means sea halo. It represents a white head. It is interesting, in the Scriptures, that white or gray hair has a reference to wisdom.

Proverbs 16:3 *"Gray hair is a crown of splendor; it is attained in the way of righteousness."*

Proverbs 20:29

"The glory of young men is their strength: and the beauty of old men is the gray head" (wisdom).

> Our Founding Fathers known for their godly wisdom created the founding documents of our nation based on the Holy Word of God.

The bald eagle as a symbol to America is a profound bird.

35

Our Founding Fathers known for their godly wisdom created the founding documents of our nation based on the Holy Word of God. They paid the price in sacrifice and life to give us their wisdom and knowledge. The white hair of the eagle represents this beautiful strength and majesty that the whole world recognizes as America's wisdom.

The 'bald' (sea) represents the nations. Our wingspan stretched over the seas to other nations to bring freedom. One of the greatest spans that America's churches provided, that literally changed history, was our missions programs! We went into the world fulfilling The Great Commission.

Matthew 28: 18-20

"Then Jesus came to them and said, "All authority in heaven and on earth has been given to me. Therefore go and make disciples of all nations, baptizing them in the name of the Father and the Son and the Holy Spirit, and teaching them to obey everything I have commanded you. And surely I am with you always, to the very end of the age"

As I begin to relate this parable of the molting eagle you will see a prophetic word emerge that will show, more than ever, that we need to pray for America. You will see clearly that the Church needs to come out from among them to pray, fast, and put Jesus as the center of our lives again.

When you look at specific parts of an eagle you learn some amazing facts.

• Eyesight:

An eagle's eye is about the size of a humans, but its sharpness is at least four times that of a person who has perfect vision! Simply put they can see clearly for miles! They are known for their expert skill in the hunt and rarely miss the capture of their prey.

• Voice:

The voice of an eagle is important because they do not have vocal cords. They produce a loud high pitched shrill. Their call is a reinforcement of the bond between other eagles, and a way to warn other eagles and predators that the area they are in is defended! It is said the eagle was used as a national emblem because, at one of the first battles of the Revolution (which occurred early in the morning) the noise of the struggle awoke the sleeping eagles on the heights and they flew from their nests and circled over the heads of the fighting men, all the while giving vent to their raucous cries. "They are shrieking for freedom," said the patriots.

• Beak:
The beak is a strong weapon. The way it was created causes a scissors effect. It allows the eagle to cut their meat.

• Talons:
The talons are very important to the eagle. He uses them to hunt and for defense purposes. They can open and close at will and can grab and hold onto prey way too big for them. The talons are weapons that other birds stay away from.

When you look at the Great Seal of The United States you find the eagle as the central figure. It shows an eagle rising. In the eagles right talon is the olive branch (peace offering). In its left talon the eagle holds the power of war, symbolized by thirteen arrows. On the beak is a scroll that says, "E Pluribus Unum" (out of many one). In the Church our motto is, "Out of ONE (Jesus) many! The eagle on the Great Seal is to represent liberty and freedom. We know that there is true freedom only through the shed blood of Jesus Christ and man receiving His sacrifice for our salvation. As a prophetic symbol God has shown the world His great love for our nation and we are considered the leader of the free world.

Jesus as the head of the Church offers the olive branch of peace to everyone who will receive Him. He also says He gives us all the power over all the power of the enemy!

(2) "Eagles Masters of the Sky" Editor © 1997 Published by Voyageur Press, Inc. Maude M. Grant

The Gathering of Eagles

Chapter 3

THE ABILITIES OF THE EAGLES

Isaiah 40:31

"But they that wait upon the Lord shall renew their strength; they shall mount up with wings as eagles; they shall run, and not be weary; and they shall walk, and not faint."

In History there are times of desperation and the Word of God is needed for powerful change and hope to take place. If there ever was a time for a Word and eagles from God for America it is now! If there ever was a time when our government needed eagles in leadership it is now. If there ever was a time that you need to know an eagle it is now. We need a touch from God! We need to see His power and glory again in this nation and in the Church. If there ever was a time when people you are familiar with and seem to know so well, but have never recognized them for who they are in Christ, it is now!

In order to understand this prophetic time for America I must give you a little history of the eagle. As I have studied eagles I have come to understand that people will become 'eagles' because they recognize the voice of the Eagle, Jesus. God has placed within our midst, as a Church the voice of Jesus through the Word. We speak the Word in power and demonstration of the Holy Spirit.

The Holy Spirit gave me a commission to write. So here we go.

VISION

I want you to get the full impact of what God has been speaking to me. Scientist say that eagles can look into the sun. It invigorates their eyes. A human would find their eyes damaged by looking into the sun. As they fly they will look literally into the sun, but it stimulates them. Thank God, that we have a Master that we can look to that can stimulate the eyes of the believers and the eagles! Psalm 119:18, *"Open thou mine eyes that I may behold wondrous things out of thy law."* The eagle can fly thirty to forty miles per hour and can see a prey at 1,000 ft. in a three square mile radius. They can fly up to 10,000 feet high and see prey when they are just soaring. They have eyes that see forward and sideways all at the same time. They can focus in either direction perfectly. It is absolutely amazing to have one hundred per cent peripheral vision looking forward or sideways. That is why they can span the whole area. God has equipped them with the power to see.

In the Bible the eyes are used in Scriptures to understand the perception of God. We have many sayings giving an idea of perception. When someone is really good at what they do people say, "Oh, he has an eye for it." If you want someone to be careful you might say, "Keep your eye on the ball." When we choose to ignore advice it is said, "You have turned a blind eye." Eyes show us an understanding in the Bible of how important it is to see. God wants us to see clearly.

Knowing the eagle can see like it does is an example for us to ask God to open our prophetic eyesight and help us to be eagles with spiritual vision. If we were to look into the sun it would blind us, but an eagle is invigorated and stimulated by something that would leave us helpless and sightless. The eagle has membranes on its eyes that every three to four seconds cleans the lens and the retina. Think about this, as a people, God has created a way to cleanse your vision through the blood of Jesus Christ. We can look directly to His Son and have greater understanding and greater insight! Looking to the Son stimulates the believer.

Vision is one of the most important things God has given. The Church should have vision to see what the Holy Spirit is saying. The Holy Spirit is constantly revealing the prophetic ministry of Jesus. America should have the vision God gave to the Founding Fathers to make us the Eagle for the World. They understood the Word for America. In Proverbs 29:18 it says, *"Where there is no vision, the people perish..."* Like the eagle, the Church must have a vision for its people and its people must have a vision for their communities, cities, and their country.

Like the eagle we must be able to see deep into the future and capture what is needed for greatness. The Church has been given the cleansing of the lens, like the eagles, through the power of the Holy Spirit and the knowledge of the Word of God. The cleansing comes through the blood of Jesus.

When God gives you incredible eyesight it is to see His plan, His greatness, His healing, His promises, and His purposes, to be fulfilled in the earth.

God has equipped us and we need to look for those lost souls the way soaring eagles fly. They have the ability to look forward and sideways. They can see under water, on the surface of land, and in the sky. They have a view of everything and the Church should be soaring for the lost like the eagle does. We need to be looking everywhere to find the souls God wants brought into His Kingdom.

In the natural, looking into the sun as an eagle does, is not a good idea, but looking to the *Son* is what is expected of us as believers. Our supernatural vision comes when as Psalm 119:18 says, *"Open thou mine eyes, that I may behold wondrous things out of thy law."*

Ephesians 1:18 states, *"I pray that the eyes of your heart may be enlightened in order that you may know the hope to which he has called you, the riches of his glorious inheritance in his holy people."*

When God gives you incredible eyesight it is to see His plan, His greatness, His healing, His promises, and His purposes to be fulfilled in the earth. The eagle and man, as God's creation, have something in common astounding vision!

WING SPAN AND FEATHERS

Eagles have a wing span of seventy to ninety-two inches, over 7,000 feathers and they can stand thirty-seven inches tall. They are huge and magnificent. It's amazing what the eagle can do. They hold their head back and that's why they look at you and they are not the least bit afraid. They can go 10,000 feet in the air and know exactly where they are and where they are going. They are not intimidated by any other kind of bird.

Their bones are hollow for one purpose, not to be weak, but to be swift. Being hollow the wings are designed aerodynamically to be able to see a fish at 1,000 feet in and beneath the water. They can hit the water and come out of the water because they are one of the most incredible birds that swim. I had never thought before about the eagle as a swimming bird. They can hit the water, get their prey, come up out of the water, and if they sink into the water they can swim with their prey. Generally, they grab their prey with their talons and just take them. They can see them at 1,000 feet just as clear as you look at someone face to face.

The eagle is one of the most amazing birds and can live to be over seventy years old. When they get about five years old they start turning white-headed, their neck becomes white, and their tail feathers all turn white. When this whitening happens it is a sign of maturity in the eagle. It is the sign that they are at the place where they can reproduce. America has gone through this same process of maturing. We have a God given gift of democracy and we want to reproduce this gift to the world. We have set goals for feeding the poor, helping the oppressed, and sanctuary to the homeless. America is losing sight of the goals the Word of God teaches us to hold up strong. *"For I was an hungered, and ye gave meat: I was thirsty, and ye gave me drink: I was a stranger, and ye took me in"* (Matthew 25:35). The Church is the hope of the world.

The feathers are the covering of the eagle, but the blood of Jesus is the covering of the believer. The constitution, like the feathers of the eagle, are the covering for America. The Word of God is the compass and covering for the believers. The strength of the eagle is a great picture of the Church and America.

A very interesting thing about the eagle is that they don't always mate every year. They only mate for the necessity of reproduction. When an eagle picks their partner it is for life. When they do mate they usually lay three eggs, three or four days apart, sometimes a week. If the first egg is a female it is the first one born. God has put within the eagle the ability to accept what is happening. In our lives parents have that divine nature to protect their children. America, with their foundation in the gospel, has that parenting nature to protect the abused and maligned people of the world.

I have often thought about going to the graveyard and seeing graves of every size. You know that God still has a plan, an eternal plan for every one of us. He says that if the sparrow falls He knows about it. He knows when those little eaglets are no longer there. God in His miraculous wisdom has created a balance with the eagle's reproduction process. It is amazing! That is why they are a protected bird in the United States. So if the eagle lives seventy years that is three score and ten years. This is a beautiful picture of God's promise to man. He promises man, also, three score and ten years. *"The days of our years are threescore years and ten; and if by reason of strength they be fourscore years, yet is their strength labor and sorrow; for it is soon cut off, and we fly away"*(Psalms 90:10). Like the eagle we take flight at the end of our days, but we are only soaring higher and starting a new eternal purpose in God's Kingdom.

In God's plan with the eagle something unusual begins to happen when they are about thirty to forty years old. They go through a molting stage. They have lived and survived, they have been fed, hunted, and reproduced. They literally have lived out God's divine plan for them. They have soared in their lifetime to a height of 10,000 feet. They are happy, moving, flying, and just being regal.

Church we like the eagles, as believers, need to live a life that finds joy in the Lord, moves as He leads us, soar looking for the hurting and lost, and entering into the royal priesthood He has made us to be. As we behold the eagle we see the majestic beauty Jesus talked about when He said, "Behold the birds of the air…" (Matthew 6:26).

Chapter 4

THE MOLTING TIME

Now the time in their life for molting comes. When this molting comes it is devastating. I want to take some time here to tell you about this stage. Molting lasts about one hundred and fifty days and it usually occurs around thirty to thirty-five years of age of the eagle.

The first thing that begins to happen is they lose all their feathers and it starts at the head and moves down to the feet. Every morning they fluff themselves up. All the beauty and practical purposes happens as they insulate themselves to adapt to the weather of the day. They have the ability to get up with great power, lift off, and to go and do whatever they want. All of a sudden things begin to crater in on them. Their feathers fall out. The beauty they had seems to totally disappear. It just seems like everything has gone wrong. This once majestic, beautiful, bird appears to look like a turkey!

I believe every Christian goes through this molting process. Sometimes it is a marriage issue, health issue, financial, or so much more. We find ourselves hurting, wondering, and even fearful of things we can't seem to control. The loss we feel, the trial, the struggle, becomes too much for us to handle.

When eagles start losing their feathers they can't fly anymore. They become weak. They want to go up and soar, but they can't. When the molting process begins and the feathers are lost, this great eagle that once soared, now has to walk and takes on itself the image of a turkey. They no longer have the ability to get up and do what they used to. Life has changed drastically for them!

This process, I have also seen in different lives of people and even in the growth and development of the Church. As I looked and observed this process I have asked the Lord, "What is this?"

Do you realize the molting stage always begins in the valley? When they have been in the high mountains now they find themselves in the low valleys. They become very vulnerable, hurting, and weak.

Psalm 23:4, *"Yea, though I walk through the valley of the shadow of death, I will fear no evil: for thou art with me: thy rod and thy staff they comfort me."*

I thought about David, as a shepherd, and wondered if he didn't watch the eagles and see them go through this molting stage. He might have said, *"God we are like these eagles going through the valley of the shadow of death, but thy rod and thy staff they comfort me."*

The most amazing thing to me is that in this molting stage they lose their vision! Sometimes trial and pain causes us to give up hope. When we lose hope we look to ourselves and give up on the Word of God in our lives. We have to remain faithful to His Word because He promises He will never leave or forsake us.

Can you even imagine where you could be soaring every morning just catching the wind, soaring to the highest heights, seeing for miles all at once, knowing that you will never want for anything? Knowing that you would always have the ability to produce for yourself and catch the prey that you need to survive? Now you have come to the place where you are losing your feathers, to the place where you are in the valley of the shadow of death, and then, all of a sudden, you get to the place where you can't even see. Your vision leaves you! What a terrible state the eagle and the believer is in when they are going through hard times.

I have seen so many church people lose their vision. Proverbs 29:18 tells us, *"Where there is no vision, the people perish: but he that keepeth the law, happy is he."*

Eagles know they have to have their vision. They know the change has taken place when they look to the sun and it no longer stimulates their eyes, but hurts them. When you are losing your vision there are always people who will come along and cloud your vision even more. The very vision God had given to you they will bring clouds to darken the vision for you. They will discourage you.

When you go to church and you are looking for a place you can come and be refreshed it will seem like every time you go to church it will get worse because of the lack of vision. When you try to ask questions, or try to share some of the things you are going through it seems all they do is hurt you. You become more vulnerable than you every wanted to become in your whole life.

America is in a molting stage. I believe because the Church no longer sees who they are in Christ. They have let the things of the world choke out the Word and the strength they used to have. *"He also that received seed among the thorns is he that heareth the word; and the care of this world, and the deceitfulness of riches, choke the word, and he becometh unfruitful"* (Matthew 13:22).

In this molting stage you don't have an appetite. You don't even want to eat. You don't want to come to church. You don't want to hear the Word of God. You don't want anything because you feel like you are going to die!

Everything anyone has said to you hurts. They have clouded your vision that God gave you. When you could soar, when you could fly, when you had the strength to help they needed you. Now you are in this molting state and they don't need you, but you actually need them, and they discourage you. Sometimes the heartbreaking trials of life make it hard for you to trust others, but you must because you usually can't help yourself in this stage of life. It can be hard, but it won't last forever. We need each other at these times in our lives.

You don't want to hear what they have to say and you don't want to eat or break bread with them. It is a sad truth, but when Christians lose the desire to eat and consume the Word of God it's because they are hurting. The vision, they believe, is gone that God has given them.

Our Founding Fathers had great vision. We find it in the *Declaration of Independence, The Constitution, The Bill of Rights,* and even in the music sang in our beginnings, like *God Bless America.*

When we use the word moral in front of compass it is an indicator of a personal belief system and your actions follow that path. It tells us what is right and wrong.

The molting is seen in America by civil unrest, abortion, crime, lack of strong moral leadership, and like the catch phrase, "Just do it," our country has lost its moral compass. A compass is a very simple instrument that will always face north in a consistent manner when a walker is out seeking direction and turns that way. When we use the word moral in front of compass it is an indicator of a personal belief system and your actions follow that path. It tells us what is right and wrong.

America cannot seem to find its original moral compass in its molting stage. We have changed the Christian marriage concept of one man and one wife. Single parents with children has become a major problem and abortion on demand is the general consensus. We have lost our feathers, vision, and strength!

In this molting stage there is a calcium that builds up on the eagle's beak. The calcium gets heavy on the beak, remember they can't see, they don't have any feathers to fly, and they have all these discouraging words from the other eagles that are flying, "Why don't you fly? What's wrong with you? Come and go with me, let's go fly."

Well, they can't fly! It seems that all the heaviness comes upon their beak. The calcium deposit grows and comes out to the very end of their beak. As they look down on their feet, as best they can, the calcium build up is on their claws. It starts increasing. Now they can't fly, they're in the molting stage, they are ugly, and they are undesirable. There are other eagles in the molting stage in the same valley that they are in, and they are trying to kill them! They're picking at them. They're hurting them. They are in the same valley and they are looking for someone to blame. The calcium deposits get so heavy that their head drops. Where they use to look up for the opportunity to soar now they are walking like a turkey. Now they're in pain and they're hurting. When they flap their wings the mighty wind no longer captures their feathers because they are gone. The pain gets so bad that they have to take this calcium deposit on the beak and pluck out any remaining feathers because of the pain.

Believe God is still with you!

Psalm 34:18, *"The Lord is near to the brokenhearted and saves the crushed in spirit."*

2 Corinthians 1:3-4, *"Blessed be the God and Father of our Lord Jesus Christ, the Father of mercies and God of all comfort, who comforts us in all our affliction, so that we may be able to comfort those who are in any affliction, with the comfort with which we ourselves are comforted by God."*

You may have taught Sunday school for thirty years. You may have done wonderful things for God and it seems like no one wants you anymore. All they want to do is pluck and pick at you. They do nothing but discourage you. This is a terrible state to be in. You may be in a molting stage and it's not what you did wrong, but what you did right! It is a time in your life that you can feel the presence of the Lord, if you will allow yourself too. Sometimes our misery is so strong we feel weak and hopeless. The eagle finds a God given solution.

The eagle will begin to peck on the rock. He tries to find a place where he can hit his head and beak so hard that he can break that calcium off. When he gets his beak cleaned he looks at his feet and he literally has to take his beak and break the calcium deposits off his nails so he can have repair to his talons.

You have to be able to cast off vain imaginations and submit your mind to Christ. You have to be willing to decide to allow change to come into your life. You must change your thinking from self-pity to the mind of Christ.

2 Corinthians 10:5, *"Casting down imaginations, and every high thing that exalteth itself against the knowledge of God, and bringing into captivity every thought to the obedience of Christ;"*

An eagle has a choice and so do you, as a believer. Just because you are an eagle doesn't mean that you don't have to help yourself. You have to make up your mind you will live and not die! You have to make up your mind that you are the blessed seed of Abraham. Just because someone doesn't agree with you should not cause you to lose your vision.

Just because your head is heavy, because of the calcium deposits, (lies and threats of the enemy), and you can't lift up your head, it hurts to look up into the sun, that used to invigorate your eyes doesn't mean there isn't a solution. It is so painful to think about pulling out the feathers that used to make you soar. After the eagle beats the rock he is at a place where he says, "I don't want to live. I'm ready to give up." The other eagles see this stage of depression, in this valley of death, which they all are in. They intensify the pecking. They intensify the hurt. They intensify the pain. They are trying to get the one that soared the highest to lay over on its back, so they can kill it.

There are people reading this book who are saying to themselves, "I am willing to lay over on my back and quit." Let me tell you something I hope you can hold on. Your finest hour is about to come! The greatest miracle of the molting eagle is that he has been molting for three months and into the last part of the molting stages, he finds himself a rock. As he goes walking with the turkeys and going through all this pain, pecking, and trying to clean his beak and claws, and he doesn't have any feathers, His feet still hurt, he still walks like a turkey, but he finds a rock or somehow makes it back to his nest.

Our Rock is Jesus Christ and He told us to cast our cares upon Him. 1 Peter 5:7, *"Casting all your care upon him; for he careth for you."*

Matthew 9:36, *"When he saw the crowds, he had compassion on them, because they were harassed and helpless, like sheep without a shepherd."*

Matthew 14:14, *"When he went ashore he saw a great crowd, and he had compassion on them and healed their sick."*

No matter how stressful your situation is cast it upon the Lord. He will deliver and set you free to soar again. He is your Rock!

Don't Quit a miracle is on its way!

Chapter 5

FALL ON THE ROCK

The eagle finds his rock. He spreads himself out over this rock because he has selected it, where the sun shines directly upon it. The eagle, in the heat of the day, all day long, will lay on that rock with his wings and what feathers he has left and embrace that rock. The sun beats down upon him and restores his feathers, restores his sight, and restores his strength. When believers bathe in the Son light of His presence they are renewed. When we as believers pray and wait upon the Lord we get restored. When the eagle is spread out over the rock, going through this pain, hurt, agony, loss of appetite, loss of sight, built up calcium, no feathers, no way to even hunt, no way to provide, no desire for anything, but maybe to die. When he is hung out over this rock he feels stronger. Because of the sunlight he begins to cry and it seems hopeless. He's hungry and he wants something to eat, but has no way to get it. He wants to soar again, but he can hardly look up. So he begins to cry. As he cries God hears him. God says, "That's my eagle."

Psalm 18:6, *"In my distress I called upon the Lord, and cried unto my God: he heard my voice out of his temple, and my cry came before him, even into his ears."*

Matthew 11:28, "Come unto me, all ye that labour and are heavy laden, and I will give you rest."

The most amazing thing happens when the eagle begins to cry, when he's given up, and laid out upon the rock. He is totally dependent on the rock. This is the place his life begins again!

We must get totally dependent on the Rock of our Salvation. The Rock of Jesus. When we pour out our self into Him it's like the eagle. We come to the place of complete surrender.

Jesus had His molting experience in The Garden of Gethsemane. There is a famous picture of Jesus leaning on the rock and praying through the night. God is sensitive to our cries. It is the place His final request came forth, "Not my will, but your will be done." He knew what was awaiting Him and instead of trying to avoid it, He knew the Father loved Him and had a divine purpose for it. We reap what He sowed for us in our times of crying out to Him.

America is just now feeling the pain of molting. As the eagle poured out himself and began to cry, he looked up and the ones who had gone through the molting stages, the ones that were familiar with the pain, began to circle him. They would come down and do aerobatics to encourage him. They would come down and bring food and drop nourishment to him. What starts to take place is, **"The Gathering of the Eagles."** The eagles do not gather unless they hear the cry. Because the cry speaks, "I want to live and not die!"

America's cry that God promises to answer is:

2 Chronicles 7:14, *"If my people, which are called by my name, shall humble themselves, and pray, and seek my face, and turn from their wicked ways; then will I hear from heaven, and will forgive their sin, and will heal their land."*

The cry tells the other eagles, who have already gone through the process, that the eagle is getting his vision back. The cry speaks, "I'm hungry again for the Word of God." The cry speaks, "I'm holding onto the Rock. No matter what has happened I am holding on! I'm basking in the Son light of His presence. I'm looking for a place where I can be in the presence of Jehovah. I have a cry that I have never cried before because I have never been in this situation before. I've never gone through the molting stages, I've never been hurt like this. I've never not been able to get up and soar. I've never not been able to provide for myself."

Because of the cry, because of the eagle, (believer) expressing that they need help, the eagles begin to gather!

> The gathering of the eagles is what the Church and America needs right now. A leadership based on the foundations of our Christian values…

They begin to circle. They begin to drop food on purpose as the ravens did with Elijah. God gave them a command. They were servants to God's prophet and they were faithful when the brook was drying up in his life. God has faithful servants he will call out to help you in your drought days. He is faithful and many who have been through the process are able to help and stand with you.

There is another interesting thing that happens to the eagles. The only ones that God commanded to gather were those who had already gone through the molting stage. If you think that somebody's going to understand where you are at and never have been through the molting you are mistaken. The gathering of the eagles is what the Church and America needs right now. A leadership based on the foundations of our Christian values and beliefs in the liberty that is promised first in Scriptures, *"If the Son therefore shall make you free, ye shall be free indeed"* (John 8:36).

The reason that the young eagles didn't bring any food was because they had no need of anything. They had never experienced the need of molting. They think, "Oh just let them die." The Holy Spirit said to me, "With where I've placed you, and with what I have called you to do, if you will teach this generation of eagles that have never been through the molting stage, to hear the cry of the one on the Rock, everyone will have every need met." We have to teach this generation to recognize the cry of the one who is sitting twenty-four inches by them, even though they have never experienced it."

James 1:27, *"Religion that is pure and undefiled before God, the Father, is this: to visit orphans and widows in their affliction and to keep oneself unstained from the world."*

Hebrews 13:16, *"Do not neglect to do good and to share what you have, for such sacrifices are pleasing to God."*

1 John 3:17, *"But if anyone has the world's goods and sees his brother in need, yet closes his*

heart against him, how does God's love abide in him?"

As they feed the eagle who is laid out depending totally upon God, the ones who have gone through this stage prepare a way and are compassionate. They begin to gather. They will all go out, hunt, and bring back food to those eagles laid out crying on the Rock. So that generation will not lose the wisdom, knowledge, and understanding that the younger eagle has never experienced. It is God's plan for them to have thirty more years. It is God's plan that you don't give up. It is God's plan for you and me to have the best years we have ever had. The molting is about to stop, and new vigor and vision is about to begin!

There's a gathering of the eagles, strong believers, which are coming to the Church and America. It is going to be one of the most exciting things you have ever seen, because God has given us the revelation of the molting eagle. The younger eagles will drink up the wisdom you gained through the molting process. They will devour it in a way that you have never seen before. They will be so hungry. You are called by

God to get up, lay on the Rock (Jesus), cry out, and wait for the gathering of the eagles to help restore you.

Here's what I believe the Holy Spirit is showing me, as this eagle began to strengthen himself, with what was gathered for him, by the gathering of the eagles, as he allowed the sunlight and the presence of God to come into his life again, at the age of thirty to thirty-five years old, he began to raise his head back up. His vision came back, his claws became brand new, his beak becomes better than it ever was. His vision improved because of the molting, when someone said something, he saw through the problem.

When the vision that had almost perished became a living thing before his very eyes he began to raise his wings and he began to strengthen himself with the new grown feathers. He looked down at his feet and they were beautiful. More powerful than they ever had been before. The gathering of the eagles, (unity), brought the solutions and the answers that met the needs. Isaiah 52:7 shows this example for us, *"How beautiful upon the mountains are the feet of him that bringeth good tidings, that publisheth peace; that bringeth good tidings of good, that publisheth salvation; that saith unto Zion, Thy God reigneth!"*

Maybe you see the eagle on the rock crying and desperate, it could be your son or daughter, your parents, your mate. Sin can bring devastation into lives, but finding the presence of God in forgiveness and clinging to the Rock can bring a miracle back into their lives.

As the eagle looked at his wings, which are sometimes ninety inches wide, and he saw the new growth, new feathers, and the beauty of the newness of the molting; he began to stand in the midst of the valley and wait for the current of the wind. We as believers need to hear the Word of God fresh again, pray, and trust Him with all our hearts.

The eagle practiced day after day with his new wings. He began to see the other eagles that had gathered, they would swoop down, and cried to him, "Come, Come on, you can do it." As he began to strengthen his wings all of a sudden there was a mighty gust of wind that came in the midst of the valley. His feathers caught the wind, and lifted him off the ground! He looked around and said, "I'm flying and I'm strong again. I'm more beautiful than I ever was before. I'm more powerful because I have the wisdom of the molting and I have laid it all upon the Rock! It's not my idea, but it's His idea. It's not my vision it's His vision."

He comes up off the ground, and he looks back at the valley that he was once in. Now he has a clear picture. There was his old feathers. There was the old calcium that came off his beak. There was the old path that he walked like a turkey on. He looked back and said, "I'll never return, but I will soar with greater wisdom, greater power, greater understanding, and greater vision. I will help those who haven't gone through the molting stage to be restored. To those who are in molting I will bring the meat. I will bring the nourishment. I will be the one who does the aerobics. I will be the one that stands up when no one else will. I will be the one that will do what no one else wants to do. I will be the one who will be here because God said so, not because man said so."

When you lay it all upon the Rock it is not your strength that is why you can say, *"They that wait upon the Lord shall renew their strength. They will mount up with wings of eagles they'll run and not be weary and they shall walk and not faint"* (Isaiah 40:31).

A beautiful expression of this process in Scripture is found in Acts 1:6-12, After Jesus was taken up into heaven the disciples watched as he was lifted up and angels told them He was gone, but that He would come back again. Then there was the gathering of the eagles (believers) as they all went together in one accord, broken hearted to Jerusalem to pray and all went to the upper room where other believers had gathered. *"And when the day of Pentecost was fully come, they were all with one accord in one place. And suddenly there came a sound from heaven as of a rushing mighty wind, and it filled all the house where they were sitting... But Peter, standing up with the eleven, lifted up his voice, and said unto them, 'But this is that which was spoken by the prophet Joel; And it shall come to pass in the last days, saith God, I will pour out of my Spirit upon all flesh: and your sons and your daughters shall prophesy, and your young men shall see visions, and your old men shall dream dreams: And on my servants and on my handmaidens I will pour out in those days of my Spirit: and they shall prophesy. And it shall come to pass, that whosoever shall call on the name of the Lord shall be saved'" (Acts 2:1-21).*

What a beautiful illustration of the parable of the molting eagles. All the disciples were broken hearted, missing Jesus, questioning all they had seen and done with Him, and doubting themselves. As they go back to the nest an unusual thing happens. As they came together, in unity with others, helping each other to understand, and feeling the lowest of their lives, a change is about to happen. A mighty rushing wind, like the one the eagles catch to fly again, comes on every person and the great restoration begins. The Holy Spirit, the Rock, the nest, and anointing of fire falls on every hurting, struggling, down trodden believer. The restoration is complete, the power of God has come, and new life begins again! The disciples can fly again! They leave the upper room full of hope, power, and resurrection. The gathering of the eagles, in that upper room, where unity had great results, was the place God chose to pour out His Spirit!

It is with great concern that I write this book. America is in a molting stage. The covering of America is down. We used to pledge, "One nation under God." We understood who was covering us in our great country; it was God. When we removed the phrase, *In God We Trust* out of our political heritage, we as citizens began relying on military, ourselves, government, and Wall Street as the safety net and balance for America. We looked to everything, but God as our source!

We have got to pray for our country. We have got to pray for our churches. We have to be the generation that brings people to the place where they understand that God needs them and they need God! When they lose their vision lift them up. When they become downtrodden and in depression, in the molting stage, encourage them. When they are ready to give up say to them, "You can't give up. Because God wants you to be an eagle strong in your season."

The eagles when they begin to gather also begin to circle. You need to lay everything down, find the Rock, or nest and say, "I've got hope and help. I've got a desire to live. I am not the same as I was when I first came into this molting stage. I have laid it all upon Jesus. He's my Rock and my Nest. I find security, peace, safety, and love in Him." Whatever you have been going through I want you to know that there are eagles gathering and circling around you to help you and to encourage you. Look up!

Psalm 121:1-3, *"I will lift up mine eyes unto the hills, from whence cometh my help. My help cometh from the Lord, which made heaven and earth. He will not suffer thy foot to be moved: he that keepeth thee will not slumber."*

A simple parable based on the life process of the eagle can be simply applied to each one of us. Life has trials and tribulation, but we are told to believe in the *Rock of Salvation* and be assured in our molting times of life that His promises are ours to claim. John 16:33 says, *"These things I have spoken unto you, that in me ye might have peace. In the world ye shall have tribulation: but be of good cheer; I have overcome the world."*

Isn't it time you catch the wind of the Holy Spirit again in your life and SOAR? Let your strength be renewed and fly again!

The Gathering of Eagles

Chapter 6

LESSONS LEARNED

Have Clear Vision

Today, there is so much noise and advertising in the world it is difficult to stay focused. The television is overrun with commercials, almost more air time then program time! It is difficult to even see what is being advertised because of the way it is presented. Eagles fly high and can see their target at least three miles away. They are very clear on what they are seeking. What does that say to us?

Scripture says, *"Where there is no vision, the people perish: but he that keepeth the law, happy is he"* (Proverbs 29:18).

Be clear in your vision

Don't let anything else catch your eyes away from what you know is the plan of God for your life. When God created you He had a purpose in His heart. This is extremely important to understand and implement in your life. Your life is going to walk on the path of your vision. If you don't know what that vision is you are going to find yourself lost, vulnerable, and constantly changing directions.

Ephesians 1:18, *"I pray that the eyes of your heart may be enlightened, so that you will know what is the hope of His calling, what are the riches of the glory of His inheritance in the saints."*

You must understand that your heart's desires sometimes direct the path you walk. Your associations and the things you allow as part of your life have tremendous influence on you. If you keep your hearts pure and follow righteousness you will make sure you receive the blessings of the Lord and not the corrections.

As a pastor it is my deepest desire to help show you the ways of God and the path of His love. That is one of the reasons I felt led to write this book. In Habakkuk 2:3 it says, *"...And the Lord answered me, and said, 'Write the vision; make it plain on tables that he may run that readeth it.'"*

In the book of Acts Ananias was told to go to Saul, who was blinded on the road to Damascus, and to lay hands on Saul; so he could have his vision or sight back. In obedience Ananias went, did what he needed to do, and God restored vision back to Saul, who now was called Paul. Sometimes it takes others to help us see clearly like the eagle sees.

My prayer, as a pastor, is to ask God to open your eyes to see the plans and the purpose He has for you. For you to understand the plans are good and not bad, and that His love will guide you all your life, if you will let Him. You have to learn to trust in the Lord and let Him guide you on your prepared path.

Everyone has a molting process in life

There come times in our lives when the unexpected and the trials show up. Like the eagle we sometimes lose the majestic feeling and look we have been walking in. When the feathers go, the beak breaks, the flight is almost impossible, it takes the gathering of healthy eagles to help us through. God will never leave you! I know in very tough and sad situations it might seem like it, but even this is a growing stage. Isaiah 46:4, *"Even to your old age I will be the same, And even to your graying years I will bear you! I have done it, and I will carry you: And I will bear you and I will deliver you."*

Psalm 71:9 says, *"Do not cast me off in the time of old age: Do not forsake me when my strength fails."*

Like the molting process of the eagle is part of their life span, so aging is part of ours. It doesn't have to be unpleasant if we, like the eagles, stay united and help each other with honor, love, and respect.

"Bald" Eagles are unique, just like you are in God's eyes

The Bald Eagle is named for its white head or white tail, which they get around the age of five years old. It signals other eagles that they are ready to find their mate. Eagles mate for life. Actually the word "balde" is an old English word that means, "It's time to settle down." I'll be brief here, but choosing the right partner in life can be the difference between happy and depressed! Take time to seek God for your mate and don't trust your own understanding. God who formed you and fashioned you knows exactly what you need. Pray and trust Him.

So many people in the body of Christ are going through a place in their life that they have not discovered the BEAUTY that is within them. The devil has so discouraged them that they are at a point where they are ready to give up because they feel like there is no beauty in them. I want to make it clear that you are beautiful! You are beautiful to the Lord, and you are part of His coat of many colors. You are part of the body of Christ, but sometimes we get so discouraged. We feel like that molting eagle that now looks like a turkey. We tend to see ourselves as the turkey. We say, "Well, I'm just one who cuts the grass, I'm just one who sweeps the floor." I want you to know that in the simple things of life the beauty of the Lord is upon you. Put your hand over your heart and say, "Lord, I'm so thankful you made me the way you did." That is a small, but very necessary action to do to help you realize you are beautiful.

1Peter 2:4, *"To whom coming, as unto a living stone, disallowed indeed of men, but chosen of God, and precious,"*

In the Living Bible it reads like this, *"It is how we pour our self into Christ."*

> Jesus Christ was chosen by the Father to bare our sins; to bare all the hindrances and things that would come to our lives.

Come to Christ who is the living Cornerstone to God's temple. He was rejected by the people, but He is precious to God who chose Him. Jesus Christ was chosen by the Father to bare our sins; to bare all the hindrances and things that would come to our lives. When we trust in Him is how we pour our self into Christ so that He becomes the curse of our yesterday. He takes the very precious wealth of the Kingdom of God and pours it back into us, to purify us, to hold us together, at such a time as we are about to head into. Do you understand the times we are living in? Do you believe we are about to get out of this world before too long? Do you know that we are going to be raised up in the twinkling of an eye? Do you realize He is coming back for us?

I want you to decree and declare to yourself, take your mirror and hold it in your hand and say, "God made me the way I am, and I'm beautiful in Him. As long as I'm obedient to be a reflection of His beauty He will supply all of my needs according to His riches in glory through Christ Jesus."

I want you to understand how beautiful you are to Him. I want you to quit beating yourself up. I want you to quit telling yourself, "You can't." I want you to know that God needs you in this hour like never before. I believe He is about to turn America back to Him. We aren't going to be called the America that can't, but we are going to be called America the Beautiful. We are not going to be called the America trodden down, but America the Blessed Nation. We will not be called the America that is discouraged, but we will be called the America of Hope. God is putting Himself back into this nation and we are going to have a voice like we have never had before, and every corruptible thing that has been corrupted is going to be exposed. We are going to come back to God and He is going to heal our nation. Like the eagle, as he goes through tremendous change, and doesn't look so regal in that molting stage, America doesn't look so regal to the world right now, but God is going to heal our nation. It is important that we pray for our leaders. The devil does not want America to come back to the glory of God.

America will be restored like that eagle again. We will be beautiful, strong, and majestic once again. How do I know this? Because God is going to start with each one of us! As we gather together in unity to preserve the weak ones, strength will come back to the eagles, the body of Christ, and America.

What God has put within us is beautiful. God is building you up as a lively stone into His spiritual temple. You are God's holy priests. Do you know that you belong to Him and that you are kings and priests? Offer the spiritual sacrifices that please Him because of Jesus Christ.

1Peter 2:5-9, *"Ye also, as lively stones, are built up a spiritual house, an holy priesthood, to offer up spiritual sacrifices, acceptable to God by Jesus Christ.*

Wherefore also it is contained in the scripture, Behold, I lay in Sion a chief corner stone, elect, precious: and he that believeth on him shall not be confounded.

Unto you therefore which believe he is precious: but unto them which be disobedient, the stone which the builders disallowed, the same is made the head of the corner.

And a stone of stumbling and a rock of offence, even to them which stumble at the word, being disobedient: whereunto also they are appointed. But ye are a chosen generation, a royal priesthood, an holy nation, a peculiar people that ye should shew forth the praises of him who hath called you out of darkness into his marvelous light;"

There is a beauty in Jesus Christ that the world cannot see openly, but as each person comes to salvation, and is filled with the Holy Spirit that beauty becomes the believer. The world can recognize beauty offered in love, respect, and help to the hurting. His beauty in you has made you lovely to others.

It is His beauty in you shining openly before the world, family, and friends.

Chapter 7

A LIVELY STONE

I want to explain some things about the lively stone. There are few things that are so exciting to me about this topic. This lively stone has some very important things in it. To illustrate this I want you to say to yourself, "I'm going to live and not die."

To be lively means that your house has the Spirit of God living in it. I want you to be full of the Holy Spirit and I want you to understand that He lives within you. To be a lively stone means that you are going to be a holy priesthood. You are going to have a communication with God that you have never had before. The year you are in and moving forward is going to be the time of holy communication with God. Say, "I am a spiritual offering to God, because I am a lively stone that is beautiful in the eyes of the Lord. I do spiritual service to Jesus and the Father, because I am a lively stone. I am alive and He is alive in me. I have a song in my being. I am a lively stone with a new melody in my heart."

We need to have a song in our heart and a song of life in us instead of a song of defeat and death. When the eagle is on that rock or in his nest and he lets out a screech over and over I believe that is his *heart song*. He screeches and the other soaring eagles come to his rescue. It is a song of life and calls others to the cause. We are born and created to win not lose. I'm above not beneath. I'm the head not the tail. I'm blessed, and so are you!

Another thing about a lively stone is that it is full of praise. I know this sounds funny, but look at your hands as ten string instruments and get'em up! Use them to praise God! Be a lively stone of praise. Devil you are under my feet. If someone tries to discourage you raise your ten stringed instruments and shout Hallelujah! That should take care of it.

When you become a lively stone your conduct changes. When you have a downtrodden countenance the devil is happy because he captured your joy. When the devil has got your mouth and using it to pull you down he will do it until you are on the ground.

Life and death is in the power of the tongue. When you give God your tongue as a lively stone the devil no longer has it or uses it to pull you down. When we get away from the tug of the tongue, of the devil, then our countenance will change. Just like the eagle's change is taking place, as he cries out in a voice the other flying eagles understand, we cry out as a voice that is saying, "I want to live as a lively stone." Miraculously, the eagle changes and flies, never to go through that downtrodden place again. They soar! When we become that lively stone we do the same with Jesus. Then you have a cheerful and grateful heart.

Affirm yourself with the promises of the Word daily. Say, "I am strong. I am beautiful. I am blessed. I am the head and not the tail." Make sure you stay a lively stone for Jesus to use in this world, for such a time as this.

A lively stone has faith that is personal between God and them. When there is a storm a lively stone will inject faith into others. God takes such joy in us because we have a personal faith in God. It is one thing to have a relationship with God, but it is another to know that God is able to do exceedingly, abundantly, above anything we could ask, think, or even hope for. You have a personal faith with Jesus.

A lively stone has the wisdom and knowledge of God that you cannot get anywhere else. It comes from the University of Heaven, and through Christ Jesus. It comes through our Messiah, our covenant, and through our inheritance. There is no weapon formed against us that can prevent us from having wisdom and knowledge. We have a heritage with the Lord!

Isaiah 54:17, *"No weapon that is formed against thee shall prosper; and every tongue that shall rise against thee in judgment thou shalt condemn. This is the heritage of the servants of the Lord,*

This is the heritage of the servants of the Lord, and their righteousness is of me, saith The Lord."

We also know that we have a confirmation with the Father who loves us. You might be asking yourself how God can love us? He wants to take you in His hands, look you in the face, and wants you to hear Him clearly say to you, "I love you."

Well, look outside at all the beautiful creation God has made. "This is how much I love you I fed the birds while you were sleeping, the flowers were growing while you were resting, and I even watered them just for you so you could see just how much I love you. Look out to the east as the sun comes up and breaks through the tree line. I sent my Son just to show you how much I love you. As you look at the sun breaking on the right and left that's the way my people are going to be. They are not going to be held back by the things of the past. They are going to break through on the right and on the left. I will illuminate myself through them because I am a God of love."

Tell them, "That their sins are forgiven, it is under the blood of my Son, when they wonder if

I love them just have them get up early with me one morning and they will see that my mercy is new every day. When they get up and see the dew that rests upon the grass, and upon the leaves of the trees, it will remind them of the dew of Herman where the blessing flows from the mountain of God. As they see, know, and look at what I have brought to bless them with, they will surely know they are truly beautiful in me.

This year I am going to bless them and pour out blessings to them. All I ask them to do is just be a lively stone for me. I am so pleased with them because a lively stone is faithful to remind me of my love. Lord, thank you for showing me your face. Thank you for waking me up and reminding me how much you love me. Thank you Lord that I am not in a place where I can't recognize who you are. Thank you Lord for keeping me in such a time like this."

Even though the eagle gets to the place of being unrecognizable he doesn't forget that he is still an eagle. Tell them, "If they will pray and write down their supplication unto me and they will move with wisdom, knowledge, faithfulness, and the personal faith that I have put in them, it will change their countenance. If they will give me praise, through it all, I will put a spiritual song in their heart."

Let them be a spiritual sacrifice unto me and I will move every obstacle out of their way so they can glow as the stone of beauty in the foundation of the house of God. He loves us so much that he wants the very best for us.

And the Scriptures express it this way, *"...Behold, I lay in Sion (Zion) a chief corner stone, elect, precious: and he that believeth on him shall not be confounded."*

I am placing a stone in Jerusalem, a chosen cornerstone, and everyone who believes in Him will never be disappointed. That lively stone that was placed in Jerusalem is our Messiah! We are going to live with Him forever. *"But ye are a chosen generation, a royal priesthood, an holy nation, a peculiar people; that ye should shew forth the praises of him who hath called you out of darkness into his marvelous light:"* (1Peter2:9).

Another Verse I would like to Share with You

Ephesians 2:19-20, *"Now therefore ye are no more strangers and foreigners, but fellow citizens with the saints, and of the household of God; And are built upon the foundation of the apostles and prophets, Jesus Christ himself being the chief corner stone;"*

God has been creating things that He always wanted to place in the earth and that is a dwelling habitation in His people. That dwelling place is a place of beauty, a place where the lively stones are, it's a place where He can come and know that the people will praise Him. A place He can come and He knows you will lift His name up and not another.

It is a place He can come and change your downtrodden countenance to the joy of the Lord. It's a place where He can come and distribute wisdom, knowledge, and understanding. It's a place where He can have a personal relationship with His people. It's a place where He can trust because of your faithfulness, a place where you create incense, prayer, supplication, and honor to Him. You become that living sacrifice He so desires. It's a place that He has wanted in the earth, and He says, "I have placed a lively stone in Israel (my people).

That stone is about to flood our churches! That stone is about to go from the throne of God, and out of that place I call Jerusalem. So tell the people to pray for the peace of Jerusalem, because when they pray for the peace of Jerusalem there will be facets of my love come to them, because I am going to create dwelling places in the whole earth. I am going to create a place in the earth that I can dwell in. It will come from the house of Israel (Jesus).

God has a plan. There will be illuminations in the Gentile nations, in every nation of the world, the light of the gospel of the Lord Jesus Christ will shine. I am creating a lively stone in every nation. I am creating a place where I can come and dwell with my people to get rid of tradition, religion, and all that stuff of hindrance, in the body of Christ. I am going to call them out from every denomination and they are going to gather like the eagles together to worship me as lively stones. They are going to see the ways of their errors and come to me and worship me, and they are going to worship me in a way that they have never worshipped me before. The illumination of Jesus is about to come into the earth like it never has before."

I am creating a new way that most people have never thought was possible. Some people think they have it all figured out, but *I Am* is creating a way of illumination because He wants to inhabit with His people, He is going to heal their bodies, land, and nation. He says, "I have a place for you because I am coming to the house of beauty in you. Quit letting people run you down, telling you that you don't have a value. You have a value to Me!" You are part of His habitation. You'll never be the same again.

This is probably one of the most exciting times someone could live, in the body of Christ. The more you see the devil turn up the heat on Israel the more God is going to love His people. He wants to announce to you, America, that you will be great and beautiful again! He is about to inhabit America again. What was founded on Him will be restored by a people inhabiting His praise and being the living sacrifice He expects them to be.

Pray this prayer with me.

"Lord Jesus, I love you with all of my heart, all of my soul, and all of my strength. I ask you Lord Jesus to bless everything I touch. I want to be that beautiful thing that you can use for the end times.

In Jesus name." Amen

The parable of the eagle can tell us a great message of resilience, struggle, faith, the gathering of the likeminded, the restoration, of not only the eagle, but our nation, and most of all ourselves. As we look to God and cry out for His mercy He will not fail us. His love will never depart from us and He wants us to soar in the heavenlies with Him.

It's time to launch out into a new purity and holiness so His presence can restore us and inhabit us forever. His love is unconditional and greater than we could ever deserve or work for. He loves us, forgives us, fills us with His Holy Spirit and gives us an abundance of His presence daily!

The Gathering of Eagles

Chapter 8

SCARS

We have so many scars in our lives that we can't see God's will for our future. Like the eagle sometimes our scars and pain keep us from seeing a beautiful future. This might be a little hard to hear, but your scars are who you are in the natural, but not who you are in the spiritual! I want to explain this to you with a little more understanding. The Messiah still carries scars that are for your deliverance. I want to show you how His scars work for you.

When we get to Heaven we won't have a problem recognizing Him. He will be able to recognize you. Your scars will be gone! He will still carry the scars that you will see were for your redemption. You will know Him and you will be known by Him, scarless! The scars of your life have been healed and you don't need to see if they are gone. Believe it!

John 19:37, *"And again another scripture saith, they shall look on him whom they pierced."*

Zechariah 12:10, *"And I will pour upon the house of David, and upon the inhabitants of Jerusalem, the spirit of grace and of supplications: and they shall look upon me whom they have pierced..."*

Those nailed scared hands of our Savior are for your healing. We don't have to carry the scars in our lives. Our scars have turned to grace and supplications. The natural eye sees the scars on each person. For example, you can cut yourself and have a scar, but they become scars that you want to cover up. There are scars that maybe you got in a fight, a situation, a wreck, an operation, or something that is hard for you to deal with. Those scars remind you of the things you went through. Here is the point I'm trying to make, your scars are what some other people see and try to define you as, but it is not who Jesus says you are because He looks past the scars of yesterday.

Most people make their decisions out of the scar mentality of the yesterdays of their lives. They make a decision to serve God or not to serve God by their scars of the past. When you make your decisions out of your scars then you don't really understand what God has given you. The eagle is scarred in the molting stage, but he never forgets that he was made to fly and that he is an eagle.

Let me give you an illustration or another parable. Think about a seed. A persimmon seed, apple seed, or any life giving seed. In those seeds there is everything that the persimmon, apple or other seed is going to be. God, Jesus Christ, has planted you at this particular time with full availability to everything that you are supposed to be. If you let your scars destroy what God has put within you then you call Jehovah a liar. You say, "That cannot be." When the angel came to Mary, the mother of Jesus, and told her she was going to have the Seed of Christ in her womb, she had to make a decision. She said in great faith not knowing how this could be, *"Behold the handmaid of the Lord: be it unto me according to thy word..."* (Luke 1:38).

You have an inheritance that you can't see. Every person has an inheritance, because of their scars. Learn to say, "Lord, I have got to look past my scars." When you are a redeemed saint and born again the Holy Spirit comes to dwell within you. There is a knowing about you that you realize who you are. When you get saved the Holy Spirit is the eyes to your heart, and that is why He leads you, guides you, and directs you, into the pathways of righteousness. So when you receive the Lord Jesus Christ you receive one of the greatest miracles ever. When you confess Jesus as your Lord and Savior the Holy Spirit begins to show you your inheritance. He begins to teach you, the seed that you are, is going to be planted by the Messiah.

Hebrews 9:16,17, *"For where there is a will and testament involved, the death of the one who made it must be established, for a will and testament takes effect (only) at death, since it is never in force as long as the one who made it is alive."*

You don't' have an inheritance until the testator who made the will is dead. There has to be proof of their death. Like most families with grown children they think they have the inheritance all figured out when their parents are gone. I constantly have to remind my kids, "I'm still here!" When you write a will the children think they have access to "your stuff" while you are still alive. No. I can give or share, but until I'm dead they have to leave my stuff alone. They do not have the legal right to any of it until…!

Now we have the Messiah and He proved that He died for us to inherit His Kingdom. He died, they buried Him, sealed the tomb, and He rose again! We have a living Savior who died for our sins so that we could have the inheritance into the Kingdom of God. This gives us the proof that we have access to the Kingdom of God. If we have proof that we have a will, that was left for us; it is His will that you prosper, that you live and not die, healed, and provided for!

Why don't we act on the will? The answer is simple, yet complicated. We don't act and receive because we look at our scars instead of His. We see our scars and say, "I'm not worthy to receive all that righteousness, goodness, mercy, and grace. The truth every believer needs to know is that it is not what you have done, it is what He did! He has provided for you an inheritance that you are not willing to claim. You have not allowed the Holy Spirit to give you the understanding you need in your heart. So you say, "No I don't deserve that." And you are right, but it is His WILL! You don't deserve the mercy, blessings, and promises, but it is His grace for you that makes it all possible.

Some eagles in their molting stage don't make it because they lose courage and in a weak state they don't realize what was put in them when they were created. Many believers just don't see the inheritance they have been given. Their eyes are on their circumstances and not on His will for them. Thomas was a disciple with Jesus. He saw signs and wonders and saw all the supernatural things that Jesus was doing.

He had a major problem. He was a man who saw the supernatural, but he never really understood the supernatural; he only saw and believed by the natural (John 20:24-25)!

We need to know, believe, and confess the supernatural power of God in our lives for others to be able to see the Kingdom of God in us.

Many believers just don't see the inheritance they have been given.

Their eyes are on their circumstances and not on His Will for them.

"But Thomas, one of the twelve, called Didymus, was not with them when Jesus came. The other disciples therefore said unto him, We have seen the Lord. But he said unto them, Except I shall see his hands the print of the nails, and put my finger into the print of the nails, and thrust my hand into his side, I will not believe."

He didn't believe the words of his close friends and would only believe Jesus was alive if he could see His scars and touch them. Most believers today are the same. You don't want to admit your doubts because you want to enjoy the spiritual side of the supernatural. Most people cannot accept that they have been written into the Lamb's book of life. Because of the death of Jesus they have become a joint heir with Him.

They can't believe that the love of the living God, while here on earth, is blessing them, was a greater love in death, leaving them the inheritance to His will. Thomas basically told the other disciples that he didn't care what they said. He basically chose not to believe what was the truth because he couldn't see it with his natural eyes. Eight days later Thomas was with them, with the door locked. Jesus then entered and said, *"Peace be unto you."* He just stood there. The shock must have been incredible!

Like the eagle, after the molting process, and no hope is left the gathering of the eagles takes place and helps him to realize everything he was born to be as an eagle was his inheritance and is still in him. No matter what it looked like, a resurrection of his majesty was still in him waiting to be restored. Strength comes from believing you are fearfully and wonderfully created. Even though at times it doesn't look good God is not finished. He will come into your life in a way you totally didn't expect. You must have eyes of the Spirit in order to see, hear, and understand what He will say to you.

Please read this next section with the Holy Spirit giving you understanding.

You are about to experience some encounters this year and throughout the rest of your life. Your spiritual eyes are going to be opened with the reading and understanding of this eagle parable. Your eyes are going to be opened to see what the Holy Spirit is going to reveal to you. Tell my people that I am about to give them a visitation if they will look past their molting process and their scars. Satan has come against them with so many scars that they can't see what I want to do for them. He wants you to look past your scars and give Him praise. When you give Him praise it wipes out the scars. This is the reading of the will so you can move into your inheritance. You literally believe through your praise that He is The Great I AM.

Let's go back to Thomas, John 20:28, *"And Thomas answered and said unto him, My Lord and my God."*

What happened when Thomas saw the Lord as the disciples had been trying to tell him? He touched His hand and side. The Lord was clear to tell him to no longer doubt, but to believe. Now imagine that Jesus is standing in front of you and His hands are extended to you. Reach up and get ahold of His hands and know that He is about to touch you in a way, by supernatural faith, that you have not experienced before if you can only believe! God wants your spiritual eyes of belief open to the visitation of the Messiah. He is going to reveal who you are in the seed He has planted in you, so you CAN POSSESS the inheritance He has for you. Believe nothing is going to be withheld from you. Nothing!

"Lord Jesus we honor you, trust you, praise you, and you are Jehovah God, our King. We do not lack anything. I thank you for touching your people who want to receive your inheritance in Jesus' name."

For the same Spirit that dwells in my Son that raised Him from the dead dwells in you, body of Christ. And I am going to quicken your mortal bodies in such a way that you are going to start to see in the Spirit and hear in the Spirit. You are about to see visions before they happen because I am bringing you to a higher place of spirituality into a realm that you have never seen before. Listen, greater things are coming because the harvest is ready, deliverance is coming as you walk in the supernatural, and you walk in obedience to me. You will see the later rain touch the former rain and it will be like never before. For this is the harvest of the end time. "Prepare, prepare, and be ready," says the Lord.

"Jesus saith unto him, "Thomas, because thou hast seen me, thou hast believed: blessed are they that have not seen, and yet have believed."

Jesus did many miracles and said the ones who hadn't seen him were blessed because they believed. Your eyes are going to be open to the Savior from this day forward. You will not look at the scars or remember the molting process. You will look at the promise and the inheritance that God has placed within you and which you are entitled to claim, because He died for you. Your natural eyes can't see what the Holy Spirit will show you with your spiritual eyes of belief. Others will not be able to see who you are in Christ with natural eyes, but you will be able to see others and who they are with spiritual eyesight.

Your spiritual eyesight is going to lead you from this day forth and you will not move or be moved by the scars of yesterday because you are forgiven, pardoned, and covered. You are part of the covenant of God. Here is what your visitation will bring if you can believe. You are going to move in the things that you thought would be impossible. You are going to see things for your own life and others lives that you didn't realize the Lord would show you. Why? The Holy Spirt has opened your eyes so you can see who you are and if you can believe you can claim the inheritance and receive all the blessings!

If you think you have seen it all you are in the wrong place. You have to get hungry again and quit rehearsing your scars.

What I'm expecting, you must take hold of your inheritance as the Spirit shows you who you are. We are different. You are going to be known so the complete plan of the inheritance can be yours. You are going to start thinking different about yourself and other people because the scars of yesterday are removed from this day forward. You are in a blood covenant enjoined with the inheritance because Jesus has died, and He has the wounds to prove that your scars are hidden in His scars. He died so He could set everything in motion. Believe and quit talking about your scars!

When you rehearse your scars you forget who you are in your inheritance. When you rehearse your abuse and persecution you truly don't understand, like Thomas, the supernatural life of whose you are and enter into it. He is the King of my life, my Lord, my Provider, and I love Him with all my heart.

Nothing should stop you from receiving everything that belongs to you from this day forward. If He sends His angles to be ministering servants to the believers then He is thinking about you!

"And many other signs truly did Jesus in the presence of his disciples, which are not written in this book:" (John 20:30).

The disciples saw many more miraculous things that Jesus did, GET READY CHURCH! He is about to do some things that have not been recorded yet. If you think you have seen it all you are in the wrong place. We have to get hungry again and quit rehearsing our scars. I am writing these things so that those of you who will believe know that Jesus, the Messiah, the Son of God is giving you everlasting life!

Are you soaring again?

"I'm just me, full of flaws, scars, and insecurities, the one who truly loves me will see beyond them, embrace me in spite of them, and love me through them." Jesse Joseph

Chapter 9

INHERITANCE

EPHESIANS 1:18, *"I pray that the eyes of your heart may be enlightened, so that you will know what is the hope of His calling, what are the riches of the glory of His inheritance in the saints..."*

The Riches of the Glory of His Inheritance to You

When we think about the banking system we know that's where we put our money. That's where we save and prepare for the future. If one day you

115

opened an envelope and you received a letter from a banker saying a relative passed away and left you a fortune you would be speechless! Paul was praying that we would understand the spiritual bank account of God. He wanted us to receive the revelation and understanding of how glorious and spectacular this rich spiritual bank account, already in existence, is to us. Paul knew that this spiritual inheritance could touch the world for the sake of Christ. With our faith in God we are able to pass this inheritance down to our children. It allows us to be adopted into God's family as sons. We get all of the promises through Jesus Christ. Jesus is explained in Scripture to be the HEIR of all things and we are joint heirs with Him! One of the greatest parts of the inheritance is that we have a home with Him in heavenly places, and we will live with Him forever!

All the Blessings That Are Coming to You

James 1:17, *"Every good thing given and every perfect gift is from above; it comes down from the Father of lights..."*

The Father teaches us about giving and promises a blessing when we do, but the greatest giver of all is God Himself. He gave us Jesus, His only Son, to die for us so we could receive everything His Father gave Him. Now it is freely given to us. The word bless or blessed in Scripture can be translated HAPPY. To be blessed by God is our inheritance. So Scripture says the man that trust God is blessed or happy. One of the most endearing and comforting Psalms in the Bible is Psalm 34. We can be assured of happiness, peace, and comfort from God.

Psalm 34

"I will bless the LORD at all times;
his praise shall continually be in my mouth.
2 My soul makes its boast in the LORD;
let the humble hear and be glad.
3 Oh, magnify the LORD with me, and let us exalt his name together!

4 I sought the LORD, and he answered me and delivered me from all my fears.
5 Those who look to him are radiant, and their faces shall never be ashamed.

6 *This poor man cried, and the* LORD *heard him and saved him out of all his troubles.*

7 *The angel of the* LORD *encamps*
around those who fear him, and delivers them.
8 *Oh, taste and see that the* LORD *is good!*
Blessed is the man who takes refuge in him!
9 *Oh, fear the* LORD, *you his saints for those who fear him have no lack!*
10 *The young lions suffer want and hunger;*
but those who seek the LORD *lack no good thing.*
11 *Come, O children, listen to me;*
I will teach you the fear of the LORD.
12 *What man is there who desires life*
and loves many days, that he may see good?
13 *Keep your tongue from evil*
and your lips from speaking deceit.
14 *Turn away from evil and do good;*
seek peace and pursue it.
15 *The eyes of the* LORD *are toward the righteous and his ears toward their cry.*
16 *The face of the* LORD *is against those who do evil, to cut off the memory of them from*

the earth.
¹⁷ When the righteous cry for help,
the LORD hears and delivers them out of all
their troubles.
¹⁸ The LORD is near to the brokenhearted
and saves the crushed in spirit.
¹⁹ Many are the afflictions of the righteous,
but the LORD delivers him out of them all.
²⁰ He keeps all his bones;
not one of them is broken.
²¹ Affliction will slay the wicked,
and those who hate the righteous will be
condemned.
²² The LORD redeems the life of his servants;
none of those who take refuge in him will
be condemned."

A joy belongs in our inheritance and the joy of the Lord is our strength. Scripture says the person who considers the poor is blessed. Our inheritance gives us the gift of compassion for others. Those that listen and hear what the Spirit speaks are blessed. You can be happy because you can hear the direction you are to go and know that He is leading, guiding, and directing your path with joy expressed for the journey. If we keep God's Word it tells us we will be blessed and happy. Even those who must endure can be blessed and happy. There was a video of eleven men, on the news, who were beheaded for their Christian faith. These men were a great gathering of the eagles (believers). The wife of one of the men said, "I just praise and worship God that He would count my husband worthy of sacrifice. It fills me with joy in Christ." The greatest blessing we receive, and we don't realize how full and happy it really is, comes from the GRACE that Jesus gives us!

There is so Much Goodness Coming to You

Psalms 107:1, *"Oh give thanks to the Lord, for He is good; for his lovingkindness is everlasting."*

One of the greatest attributes of God is His goodness. As children of God you must accept, understand, and know you absolutely live in His goodness. It is the very foundation of who God is and a great truth few understand. When you look at the work of God in Genesis you see everything He created and He called it good. Moses asked to see God's glory and God responded, *"I Myself will make all My goodness pass before you, and will proclaim the name of the Lord before you"* (Exodus 23:19). You are about to understand the goodness of God. God is good, all the time!

You will Have Such Wisdom That People Will Come to You

Job 12:13, *"With Him are wisdom and might; To Him belong counsel and understanding."*

When you think of the wisdom of God, and the knowledge of Scripture, that tells us we have the mind of Christ it is amazing to know God is going to release this infinite wisdom as part of our inheritance. This God wisdom being released to us is far greater than man's wisdom. God knows everything about everything.

A.W. Tozer and J. I. Packer state this about wisdom, *"Wisdom is the power to see, and the inclination to choose, the best and highest goal, together with the surest means of attaining it. Wisdom is, in fact, the practical side of moral goodness. As such, it is found in its fullness only in God. He alone is naturally, entirely, and invariably wise."*

Just think about that the next time you have to make a major decision in your life. This is your inheritance.

The Mysteries of The Gospel Are Going to be Unlocked for You to Partake and Understand

This is an exciting principle to understand, basically your inheritance includes a spiritual insight that the natural man cannot understand.

"But the natural man receiveth not the things of the Spirit of God: for they are foolishness unto him: neither can he know them, because they are spiritually discerned" (I Corinthians 2:14).

The mysteries will show wisdom, understanding, revelation, and much more to questions you will have, but don't understand. As your inheritance you also gain the mind of Christ so your future is assured. You can rest assured that He is going to do what He said He is going to do. He is not man that He can lie and you will have the understanding of the assurance.

You are going to be known as you are known and have the assurance that He is able to keep what you have committed to Him. You know, that you know, that He is

We are restored and in a place of blessing when we inherit His Kingdom. If you will let God take you through your times of tribulations and trials you too can be a mountain climber again.

faithful. You are no longer looking at your scars, but now your focus is on your inheritance.

One of the greatest things He gave us was to deliver us out of Egypt (symbol of the world). Get a hold of His hands and let Him get ahold of your hands and praise Him for pulling you out of Egypt into your inheritance. You have an inheritance and He opened your spiritual eyes, put you under grace, and you are blessed in the name of Jesus!

Your inheritance is beautiful, abundant, powerful and just for you! Accept, believe, and live in it!

Once the molting process is over. Like the eagle, he leaves the ground that is holding him down and spreads his new feathers wide and takes off again. He doesn't remember the scars, he remembers the new soar!

No longer weak and tired, but renewed in strength, beauty, and knowing the mountain tops belong to him again. The eagle now understands he is back into a place of majesty and assurance of who he is and what he can do now that he is in restoration.

We are restored and in a place of blessing when we inherit His Kingdom. If you will let God take you through your times of tribulations and trials you too can be a mountain climber again. You can have a perspective from a heavenly point of view and know He is restoring you in every area of your life.

Chapter 10

SEVEN POWERS

It is easy for God to use you if you are willing! He gives everybody opportunities, but not everybody recognizes those opportunities. The natural eyes look at the hurts, pains, and struggles. Sometimes the weapons that come against us are words. The natural man knows this part of life very well. Our mindset is usually, "How can God use me, with all the hurt?" God will give every person the opportunity to walk in their blessing, promise, and gift. In order to do this though we have to be stretched or expanded out of our comfort zones. And too many people don't like the expansion. As we grow in Christ and let go of the wounds we come to that place where the inheritance we enter into helps propel us higher.

Many people won't admit they have scars, but a sure fire way of knowing they do is when someone will say something to them and they react or respond in a negative way. If you react you are reacting out of the scar or wound in your life. If you will allow yourself to respond you are maturing, growing, and changing. In order to respond you must find an intimate level with God and get really honest. Admit to God privately that what was said or done hurts. Ask God to put the healing power of His love over you to calm you and help you to forgive and let it go. We need to let are hearts be expanded and ask God to heal the areas we *react in.* When you come to the place where you respond you realize God has healed you and the joy of the Lord now becomes your strength.

I would like share with you the seven powers God has given to us in order to enjoy the inheritance and erase the scars.

Seven Powers

1. <u>Hope</u>

I Perter 1:2-5

"...Grace unto you, and peace, be multiplied. Blessed be the God and Father of our Lord Jesus Christ, which according to his abundant mercy hath begotten us again unto a lively hope by the resurrection of Jesus Christ from the dead, to an inheritance incorruptible, and undefiled, and that fadeth not away, reserved in heaven for you, who are kept by the power of God through faith unto salvation ready to be revealed in the last time."

Hope is refreshed in our lives and a knowing of God's great peace allows us to believe it's going to be alright.

2. <u>Great Power is in the Resurrection</u>

Acts 1:8

*"But ye shall **receive power**, after that the Holy Ghost is come upon you: and ye shall be witnesses unto me both in Jerusalem, and in all Judaea, and in Samaria, and unto the uttermost part of the earth.*

Acts 4:33, *"And with **great power** gave the apostles witness of the resurrection of the Lord Jesus: and great grace was upon them all."*

The love and the ability to talk about Jesus is a natural outcome of these powers in the Spirit.

3. Excellent Power
2 Corinthians 4:7

*"But we have this treasure in earthen vessels, that the **excellency of the power** may be of God, and not of us."*

Every believer is empowered with the supernatural power of the Holy Spirit.

4. Eternal Power for Your Visible
Romans 1:20

*"For the invisible things of him from the creation of the world are clearly seen, being understood by the things that are made, even his **eternal power** and Godhead; so that they are without excuse:"*

A great power given to us as believers is revelation and understanding! The wisdom of revelation, knowledge, and understanding leads us to the ability to apply the wisdom in our everyday lives. The Scriptures tell us in Proverbs that wisdom is shouting out to you and it is not hidden.

5. <u>Glorious Power</u>
Colossians 1:11

"Strengthened with all might, according to his **glorious power**, unto all patience and longsuffering with joyfulness;"

God gives us the power to handle the *hard in life* with patience and joy! There is the power of the Holy Spirit in you to KNOW that the joy of the Lord is your strength!

6. <u>Divine Power</u>
2 Peter 1:3

*"According as his **divine power** hath given unto us all things that pertain unto life and godliness, through the knowledge of him that hath called us to glory and virtue:"*

The nature of divine is now and forever more a part of your life. The world as we know it is full of corruption and we partake of the divine nature of God through the "exceeding great and precious promises in Christ."

7. <u>Exceeding, Mighty, Great Power of Glory</u>
Ephesians 1:17

"That the God of our Lord Jesus Christ, the Father of glory, may give unto you the spirit of wisdom and revelation in the knowledge of him:"

Ephesians 1:19 *"And what is the **exceeding greatness of his power** to us-ward who believe, according to the working of his mighty power,"*

You are loved and the power of God will carry you through your molting times. He carries your scars in His resurrection power. You have all these powers working for you in your times of afflictions, trials, and tribulations. These powers of God are used in you to help you to want to fly again. He wants to see His glory in you and He has marked you with His Son's blood that washes you white as snow. It's time to get up and soar in the high places again!

Chapter 11

BABY EAGLES

It takes about four years for a baby eagle to test its wings and grow up. The process can be very amusing. The birds will begin to jump up and down in the nest and flap their wings. They will eventually try to jump out of the nest to fly and because they haven't experienced fight they quickly lose altitude and land on the ground. They are probably thinking, "What do I do now? They don't wait long for an answer as the parent eagles swoop down and do a little eagle talk and walk, and they get them back to the nest again. After they rest awhile they attempt flight again and go for the height they find in a tall branched out tree. They know they are safe there.

Here is an illustration that we as believers need to learn. Little attempts to test out our strengths are what teach us how to fly.

To find our rest, safety, and launch pad in a tall tree is like turning to Jesus and knowing our safety and place of security is in our Tree of Righteousness.

We need to make sure we find our security in our Tree of Righteousness. He is rooted, grounded, and strong enough to hold us up.

Another unusual thing can happen to baby eagles and it is called 'mopping.' This is when smaller birds will call out to each other and join together to keep the larger birds from flying near their nest and their young. This is an illustration of strength in numbers! When we, as the Church, call out to each other and join hearts in prayer and praise we see the protection, healing, and power of God change the circumstances we feel too small to handle. There is strength in numbers!

Growth as a believer takes time, energy, and effort. Like the eagles the steps are learned with each jump, flight, branch landing, land landing, food hunting, and nest building. There is a preparation for each stage of growth. Jesus does the same with us, He prepares us and through the Holy Spirit He guides, trains, and grows us up. Make sure you study, pray, get into a good nest, (church) and find strength in numbers. Don't ever forget you were fearfully and wonderfully made.

His love is strong enough to get you through life's trials and tribulations. He has overcome and promised we will too! Like the Word says, *"But they that wait upon the Lord shall renew their strength; they shall mount up with wings as eagles; they shall run, and not be weary; and they shall walk, not faint"* (Isaiah 40:31).

As the eagle is a symbol for America you can begin to see all the leaps and feats of flight through the history of America we have gone through as a nation and as a people.

Red, white, and blue are the colors of our flag and I am reminded of the red in the Scripture "made nigh by the blood."

Ephesians 2:13, *"But now in Christ Jesus ye who sometimes were far off are made nigh by the blood of Christ. For he is our peace, who hath made both one, and hath broken down the middle wall of partition between us; Having abolished in his flesh the enmity, even the law of commandments contained in ordinances; for to make in himself of twain one new man, so making peace; And that he might reconcile both unto God in one body by the cross, having slain the enmity thereby:"*

It seems as though the blood of Jesus has been absent from our more recent past, but the Holy Spirit is going to cover our nation again with the blood of Jesus. The body of Christ is going to be treated totally different. There is a transfer of wealth, wisdom, knowledge, and understanding that is coming to America again through the gifts and callings operating in the body of Christ. Satan is so mad that he has lost his foothold in this nation. But we are not baby eagles any more we have learned to lodge in the Tree of Righteousness and now to bring forth His fruit.

Expect to be treated like royalty. The color purple is coming on the nation, and it is a color of royalty. America will be respected all over the world.

America will be in a position of influence and will be treated like royalty.

1Peter 2:9, *"But ye are a chosen generation, a royal priesthood, an holy nation, a peculiar people; that ye should shew forth the praises of him who hath called you out of darkness into his marvelous light:"*

You have been planted in the past, but this is the year to bear fruit. You are going from a place of being taken care of, in the nest, to flying. The parent eagles won't be picking you up and moving you around. By now you have learned to leap and take flight. You are going to become a fruitful plant. People are going to recognize you for who you are in Christ and treat you accordingly.

Sometimes, like the eagle, you feel defeated.

You might feel like a weed growing without hope, but this year you are set aside by God to do great and mighty things for His Kingdom. Satan will not stop you. You will do great things. Believe it!

Matthew 21:22

"And all things, whatsoever ye shall ask in prayer, believing, ye shall receive."

John 14:12

"Verily, verily, I say unto you, He that believeth on me, the works that I do shall he do also; and greater WORKS than these shall he do; because I go unto my Father."

America is in a position of influence and will be treated like royalty. America will have a special and unique covenant with Israel. When God calls you to come and dine with Him this is an invitation to dinner. He wants to sup with you (communicate with you), and pour out blessings on you. You will be blessed coming and going.

Deuteronomy 28:1-13
"And it shall come to pass, if thou shalt hearken diligently unto the voice of the LORD thy God, to observe and to do all his commandments which I command thee this day, that the LORD thy God will set thee on high above all nations of the earth:

And all these blessings shall come on thee, and overtake thee, if thou shalt hearken unto the voice of the LORD thy God.

Blessed shalt thou be in the city, and blessed shalt thou be in the field.

Blessed shall be the fruit of thy body, and the fruit of thy ground, and the fruit of thy cattle, the increase of thy kine, and the flocks of thy sheep.

Blessed shall be thy basket and thy store.

Blessed shalt thou be when thou comest in, and blessed shalt thou be when thou goest out.

The LORD shall cause thine enemies that rise up against thee to be smitten before thy face: they shall come out against thee one way, and flee before thee seven ways.

The LORD shall command the blessing upon thee in thy storehouses, and in all that thou settest thine hand unto; and he shall bless thee in the land which the LORD thy God giveth thee.

The LORD shall establish thee an holy people unto himself, as he hath sworn unto thee, if thou shalt keep the commandments of the LORD thy God, and walk in his ways.

And all people of the earth shall see that thou art called by the name of the LORD; and they shall be afraid of thee.

And the LORD shall make thee plenteous in goods, in the fruit of thy body, and in the fruit of thy cattle, and in the fruit of thy ground, in the land which the LORD sware unto thy fathers to give thee.

The LORD shall open unto thee his good treasure, the heaven to give the rain unto thy land in his season, and to bless all the work of thine hand: and thou shalt lend unto many nations, and thou shalt not borrow.

And the LORD shall make thee the head, and not the tail; and thou shalt be above only, and thou shalt not be beneath; if that thou hearken unto the commandments of the LORD thy God, which I command thee this day, to observe and to do them:"

The gatherings of eagles, (believers), is happening now. The Church is pulling together and we are not staying denominations, as our glue, but becoming "the saints," a peculiar people.

The Church is coming out of complacency and moving in one accord for righteousness to prevail. With our gathering together we see Matthew 16:18 demonstrated. *"And I say also unto thee, That thou art Peter, and upon this rock*

I will build my church; and the gates of hell shall not prevail against it."

This is your season to bloom. Angels are released to take care of you and our nation.

Psalm 91

"He that dwelleth in the secret place of the most High shall abide under the shadow of the Almighty.

I will say of the LORD, He is my refuge and my fortress: my God; in him will I trust.

Surely he shall deliver thee from the snare of the fowler, and from the noisome pestilence.

He shall cover thee with his feathers, and under his wings shalt thou trust: his truth shall be thy shield and buckler.

Thou shalt not be afraid for the terror by night; nor for the arrow that flieth by day;

Nor for the pestilence that walketh in darkness;

nor for the destruction that wasteth at noonday.

A thousand shall fall at thy side, and ten thousand at thy right hand; but it shall not come nigh thee.

Only with thine eyes shalt thou behold and see the reward of the wicked.

Because thou hast made the LORD, which is my refuge, even the most High, thy habitation;

There shall no evil befall thee, neither shall any plague come nigh thy dwelling.

For he shall give his angels charge over thee, to keep thee in all thy ways.

They shall bear thee up in their hands, lest thou dash thy foot against a stone.

Thou shalt tread upon the lion and adder: the young lion and the dragon shalt thou trample under feet.

Because he hath set his love upon me, therefore will I deliver him: I will set him on high, because he hath known my name.

He shall call upon me, and I will answer him: I will be with him in trouble; I will deliver him, and honour him.

With long life will I satisfy him, and shew him my salvation."

As the gathering of eagles takes place I am reminded of a Scripture, 2 Samuel 1:23

"Saul and Jonathan were *lovely and pleasant in their lives, and in their death they were not divided: they were swifter than eagles, they were stronger than lions."*

There is a divine beauty found in unity. There is a divine power released in unity, and God's speed goes before the works He wants you to perform in His name.

Psalm 33:12-15

"Blessed is the nation whose God is the LORD; and the people whom he hath chosen for his own inheritance.

The LORD looketh from heaven; he beholdeth all the sons of men.

From the place of his habitation he looketh upon all the inhabitants of the earth.

He fashioneth their hearts alike; he considereth all their works.

Psalm 133:1-3
"Behold, how good and how pleasant it is for brethren to dwell together in unity!

It is like the precious ointment upon the head that ran down upon the beard, even Aaron's beard: that went down to the skirts of his garments;

As the dew of Hermon, and as the dew that descended upon the mountains of Zion: for there the LORD commanded the blessing, even life for evermore.

The devil has been trying to attack the bodies of believers to test their testimony, but the molting stage is over! Their testimony will ring aloud like the bells on the bottom of the Ephod of the priest's garments. Those bells ringing will be saying, "You are alive! You are alive!" Be encouraged make plans for success. This is your year. This is your finest hour.

Like the eagles, America, the Church, and each individual believer have come together at this divine appointment of history to shew forth the glory of God.

Chapter 12

OBEDIENCE OVER FEAR

When the Lord called me to the ministry over fifty years ago, I was a scared person. Many people had done things that I believed were hurtful and wrong to me, and I was carrying those scars. The Lord was very clear to me that I had to get over those feelings. He assured me that those scars were not mine to carry, but they were on me and I had to get over it.

I had to get past my scars before I could be effective in God's Kingdom. So I had to let God heal and cover those scars so that I could speak clearly to you about what He wants you to do with your scars. If you continue to carry those scars you get to where you don't trust people, you get suspicious of everyone's motives, you don't trust your own judgement, and doubt God.

It really isn't easy to follow the Lord because each person has to make a decision in their own mind. That is what they must want to do. Making the decision is a hard and life changing experience. It takes time, prayer, and strength to answer the call of God in your life. Determine in your mind that you won't let anything alter you from that course. It's easy for God to use you because He is always willing. Sometimes you have to be in the right place at the right time. Everybody has opportunities, but sometimes we don't recognize those opportunities.

Our natural eyes look at the hurts because we know ourselves so well and think, "How can God use me with all that hurt?" The world wants to hurt you. Your first reaction is to never let your guard down. Learn how to fight, but you have to let the Lord put a peace in you.

Throughout the years of your walk with Him He increases the peace and your obedience to the

Word. The increased peace will bring contentment and joy to your life. It's one thing to be able to achieve something, but it is quite another to be able to keep it. It is important to put your trust and whole weight on God.

Now let me give you an illustration about change. Sometimes, if you can imagine, walking on a thin wall or floor board you can put your foot through it. That's the way it kind of feels when God has you in transition. You don't feel that real sure footing. Once you step past the uncertainty of it and put your faith, hope, and trust in Him you can wait and see what happens in peace.

We all, like the eagle, face change. Change is not easy and often not very pretty, but it is the way God chooses to stretch our wings and help us soar in faith again. Change is hard. Change comes with the unknown. Sometimes change causes great fear, but we are commanded in Philippians 4:6-9 to:
"Be careful for nothing; but in everything by prayer and supplication with thanksgiving let your requests be made known unto God.

And the peace of God, which passeth all understanding, shall keep your hearts and minds through Christ Jesus.

Finally, brethren, whatsoever things are true, whatsoever things are honest, whatsoever things are just, whatsoever things are pure, whatsoever things are lovely, whatsoever things are of good report; if there be any virtue, and if there be any praise, think on these things.

Those things, which ye have both learned, and received, and heard, and seen in me, do: and the God of peace shall be with you."

Our breakthrough is here and after reading this book I believe you will be able to see, hear, and understand what the Lord is preparing for you. What happens is that with all the scars we have in life we can't see God's will for us. What I want to do through this book is to show you that your natural eyes, on your scars, cannot keep you out of God's promises unless you let them! Whatever gives God the most glory is on His time frame. What I mean by that is that there are things that happen in our lives; sometimes the Lord adds to our lives, sometimes He takes away and we get impatient because of it. What you have to do is rely on Him to put in a blessed addition or a blessed subtraction. You have to be able to pray, "Lord whatever you don't want in me take it out. Whatever you want in me put it in." If you allow God to transition you through your molting process He will bring others to your aid and He will change you for His glory. America has just come through decades of molting. Now America has come back to a place where a pouring out is about to happen. The Lord tells us He will pour out His Spirit on us as individuals and Americans.

Joel 2:28-29

"And it shall come to pass afterward, that I will pour out my spirit upon all flesh; and your sons and your daughters shall prophesy, your old men shall dream dreams, your young men shall see visions:

And also upon the servants and upon the handmaids in those days will I pour out my spirit."

The eagle, as a symbol for America, shows us through this parable that a renewing is coming. Young men shall see visions and those that have the gift of prophecy will predict what will happen and God will perform it. God will link up arm and arm with them in dreams.

I'm excited with what God is about to do in America. He will walk with America in revelation like never before. When you understand what this means it is easy to understand a place that changes you when you get in it. Really powerful and radical faith used like never before, raising up an army, nothing can stop. The body of Christ will win souls for the Kingdom of God. That miracle alone will change the face of America. Bringing people into the wisdom of how much God loves them will cause change and life to many. This is the season for understanding the times you are living in. This is the season to prosper. This is a season when America and the Church can walk out Psalm 91.

The devil is trying to attack the body of Christ and America's testimony, but God's blessings will be like the bells on the bottom of the ephod of the priest's garments and will ring out, "They are alive, they are alive." So be encouraged and make your plans for change and have faith for promised success. This is your year and one of America's finest hours for God's blessing to pour down upon us.

Point the people back to God. Reestablish relationship with Jesus, based on the Holy Spirit, and the original documents of this land. Bring back the healing of divisions. There is no place for a racist bone in the body of Christ! Recognize the value of each person and don't be judgmental. Live within the authority given by the Holy Spirit to you so you are an ambassador for Christ.

God is going to show up conspicuously in America. No one will be able to deny that He is God. You think what you have seen before is good, but you haven't seen anything yet. Those who will not let fear get into their hearts, and stop them from the changes God is making in their lives, for His glory, will see signs and wonders.

You don't have to fight the battle anymore. The battle is the Lord's. I was always fighting the battle to answer God's call. I found out He was going to use me conspicuously as I was willing to do everything He desired from me. I let go of the fear and began to soar. Quit worrying about what it costs and let God fight the battle to get you where He has already prepared for you. Jeremiah 29:11, *"For I know the thoughts that I think toward you, saith the LORD, thoughts of peace, and not of evil, to give you an expected end."*

He expects you to rely upon Him. He sets the itinerary for your life. He knows when that time to break the calcium off your beak comes and knows you will have a Word to speak in due season. Don't give up! Go to Him for yourself. Lay aside all fears, torment, reputation, and grave clothes so you can function in conspicuous miracles.

Remember these thoughts:

- No spirit of fear, but love, power, and a sound mind.
- The media gets the watcher and nation into fear. The Word keeps you in faith.
- God's about to do something great in this nation. Not to fear anything.
- Be not afraid God is still in control of the trees, birds, fruit, and land. If He can feed the birds He can feed you.
- America has blessed my people Israel and the world and God will reward His Church and America.
- Learn to operate in miraculous faith and give up the spirit of fear. Get excited about how much God loves you. Realize He has

prepared this time in history for His children.

Revelation 5

"And I saw in the right hand of him that sat on the throne a book written within and on the backside, sealed with seven seals.

² And I saw a strong angel proclaiming with a loud voice, Who is worthy to open the book, and to loose the seals thereof?

³ And no man in heaven, nor in earth, neither under the earth, was able to open the book, neither to look thereon.

⁴ And I wept much, because no man was found worthy to open and to read the book, neither to look thereon.

⁵ And one of the elders saith unto me, Weep not: behold, the Lion of the tribe of Judah, the Root of David, hath prevailed to open the book, and to loose the seven seals thereof.

⁶ And I beheld, and, lo, in the midst of the throne and of the four beasts, and in the midst of the elders, stood a Lamb as it had been slain, having seven horns and seven eyes, which the seven Spirits of God are sent forth into all the earth.

⁷ And he came and took the book out of the right hand of him that sat upon the throne.

⁸ And when he had taken the book, the four beasts and four and twenty elders fell down before the Lamb, having every one of them harps, and golden vials full of odours, which are the prayers of saints.

⁹ And they sung a new song, saying, Thou art worthy to take the book, and to open the seals thereof: for thou wast slain, and hast redeemed us to God by thy blood out of every kindred, and tongue, and people, and nation;

¹⁰ And hast made us unto our God kings and priests: and we shall reign on the earth.

¹¹ And I beheld, and I heard the voice of many angels round about the throne and the beasts and the elders: and the number of them was ten thousand times ten thousand, and thousands of thousands;

¹² Saying with a loud voice, Worthy is the Lamb that was slain to receive power, and riches, and wisdom, and strength, and honour, and glory, and blessing.

[13] *And every creature which is in heaven, and on the earth, and under the earth, and such as are in the sea, and all that are in them, heard I saying, Blessing, and honour, and glory, and power, be unto him that sitteth upon the throne, and unto the Lamb for ever and ever.*

[14] *And the four beasts said, Amen. And the four and twenty elders fell down and worshipped him that liveth for ever and ever.*

Look at things differently, let God bring you those blessings, honor, wisdom, and power. It is not by accident that you came to a place of change. Just be obedient, let go of the fear, and trust Him. Enter into the promise that will bring you to a blessing of renewal and strength, and like the eagle look up and see the salvation of the Lord!

The Gathering of Eagles

Chapter 13

ABIDE IN HIM

I asked a question of my congregation one Sunday, "How do you tell if you are in need or you are abounding?" One of the funniest answers was, "My stomach will growl." Another answer was, "I have been successful and a failure; I had the joy of both." When you have joy in trouble the Lord is your strength. No matter what comes God is going to take care of you. My assurance is in what God says He will do.

When we have peace, Jesus left His peace to us, we can rest in that calm assurance. In John 15: 5, *"I am the vine, ye are the branches: He that abideth in me, and I in him, the same bringeth forth much fruit: for without me ye can do nothing."* We are to abide in Him and bring forth fruit. We are predestined to conform to the image of Christ, but we try to do things when we are not abiding in Him. When we abide in Him He helps us with peace.

The problem a lot of people get into is when they are trying to accomplish all things without abiding in Him; thinking they are! For example, a fan, when the power is on, cools the room and is a refreshing tool. When the power is pulled out and the fan is not connected to the power any longer it keeps rotating for a while and the powerful tool it was is becoming weak and useless. It is still spinning, but it has lost its power to be used effectively. When we are not abiding in Him we are the disconnected fan. We are running, but not in purpose.

Abide in Him and operate in His power. Do not let the opinions of others, and not what God wants you to do rob your peace and joy from you.

Philippians 4:13, *"I can do all things through Christ who strengthens me."* We try to do all things without His strength. I can do a lot, but it is not perfect or pretty. We have to abide in what He is producing through us. If you are not abiding you will have heartache and pain. We do what people want rather than abide in Him and allowing the Word to have free course in our actions. The Word of God must have free course in your life.

If you are weak it is because the Word is not abiding and having free course in your life. The devil will send assignments against you to destroy you. But you have to command them to leave and they can have no part of your purpose under Heaven. Break every agenda and allow the power of the Holy Spirit, with the Word of God active in you, to deliver, set-free, and bless you.

You can't please everyone. You will wear yourself out if you do not abide in Him. I am not regulated by what someone else thinks. I am not the tail I am the head because I do not operate in my own strength. I have been in hundreds of churches and you can't minister in a church where control and the suppression of the Holy Spirit has taken place.

The God in you is greater than your mess. He brings correction because He loves us. You can't be wishy washy with the Word of God. When it has free course you have *centurion faith*. Just send the Word into the situations and God will do it. He doesn't need you to try to sweep out all the demons. He is more than able to manifest our answers through our great faith in the Word. If you are looking for another answer not in the Word and resting on man's wisdom you are going the wrong direction.

Use the authority He has given you through His Word. The Word made you and will regulate you, strengthen you, heal you, and if God was smart enough to send the Word to make and heal you He is more than capable of handling anything you are facing. When the Lord tells you to do something, other people don't understand, you cannot be a man pleaser, you must do it. The Word strengthens you and perfects your seed. Encourage one another.

What causes division in church? John 10:10, *"The thief cometh not, but for to steal, and to kill, and to destroy: I am come that they might have life, and that they might have it more abundantly."*

The thief...devil, wants to kill you and your pastor wants to save you.

I Peter 3:22

"Who is gone into heaven, and is on the right hand of God; angels and authorities and powers being made subject unto him."

Jesus died for us and went to Heaven. He is at the right hand of God making intercession for us twenty-four/seven. He is wanting the Church to get into agreement with what He established and made possible. He came to do the will of the Father.

Why are we in such turmoil most of the time? We are not abiding in Him. I John 2:28, *"And now, little children, abide in him; that, when he shall appear, we may have confidence, and not be ashamed before him at his coming."* He said, *"I am the way, truth, and life,"* He told us to follow Him and His words. As a body of believers we look to Jesus and say, "I want to be like You." Jesus will correct me, when I make mistakes, because He loves me. I don't have time to find fault with my brother and sister. Christ must dwell in your hearts by faith in love.

As we consume the Word He will consume us and abide in us. You can be free in Christ. In America we need to realize that it is only the Word in us, being brought into demonstration of His Spirit, which will make America great again. We need to vote according to the Word not party. We need to live according to the Word not our selfish wants and desires. We need to have compassion for one another by the Word of God, and we will help and restore faith to the poor and helpless. We have to raise our children according to the Word in order to raise up righteousness in this nation.

America has gone through its molting process, the Church has gone through a molting process, and now it is time to make the Word alive, active, aware, and alert in order to bring the changes that will cause us to go beyond anything we can hope, think, or ask for.

Our weapons of prayer, the Word, and grace will pull down the strongholds in our nation and our lives. He is more than enough for us to meet the needs of our country and our families.

In this world I am not afraid of man. I am not ashamed of the gospel of Jesus Christ. Being in the ministry, answering the call over forty years ago, has taught me there is no reason to wait for Heaven it is right here, now!

Jesus says enter in He has finished the work. We just have to abide in Him and the Word. Fear is no longer any part of our lives.

Chapter 14

PROPHECY FOR HIS EAGLES

The time is coming when men will not endure sound doctrine. What I am doing with you this hour, in this book, is to give you the truth; so you can pray your brothers and sisters out of discontent, unbelief, and faithlessness. So I am appointing you to the ministry that you have been called to and now you have the Spirit of the evangelist upon you.

You, God, are our living hope and it is your presence that we long for. I have seen how much you love us and my heart has enlarged to hold your glory and love for me.

It is when we recognize the presence of the Lord that the Holy Spirit comes and dwells within us to lead, guide, love, protect, and call us His own. There is nothing in this world that you will be able to compare to His glory. There is nothing is this world that you will desire more than His unconditional love. There is nothing that can replace Jesus in your life. His presence is what causes you to shine in God's glory.

In His presence you are so protected and it is in His divine presence you feel a love, and fall in love, past the experience the natural mind can comprehend. Just fall in love with Jesus. Learn to trust Him. Learn to understand He wants the best for you and sometimes that means we must make changes. We are never going to be alone and He will never leave us in a damaged mindset. He heals, restores, and commissions us for greatness in His Kingdom.

He brings in His love for one another. God is almighty and holy. He is so worthy for us to live in praise and worship of Him. Let your hearts soar in worship higher than ever before. Sing out a new song and show Him He reigns in your heart because He is Holy.

It's time to set your mind on listening very closely to what the Holy Spirit will speak to you. Your ears and heart must hear! He has promised you to pour out His Spirit and that will bring renewal in your life and healing. He will open the windows of Heaven for you. He will pour out a blessing so great you can hardly contain it all. Let Him flood you with all of His mercy, love, and grace.

Ephesians 2:8, *"For by grace are ye saved through faith; and that not of yourselves: it is the gift of God:"*

Realize this salvation gift is only given to us by God's beautiful grace and it is freely given. God sacrificed His Son just for you; accept Him, live for Him, worship Him, and serve Him with your whole heart, mind, spirit, and strength!

Take a second to just realize that out of every person on the face of the earth He calls you by your name and knew you before you were ever born. He knows what you need and will meet those needs. Let Him change you for His purposes, plans, and future. He doesn't make mistakes. You are loved, chosen, and made for His glory. Let Him be the love of your life. Let Him be the value to your everyday walk. He is your hope and there is nothing He will not do for you. I know sometimes the hurts and pains of life are hard to bare, but He will not abandon you. You will fly again!

Colossians 1:1-14

"Paul, an apostle of Jesus Christ by the will of God, and Timotheus our brother,

2 To the saints and faithful brethren in Christ which are at Colosse: Grace be unto you, and peace, from God our Father and the Lord Jesus Christ.

3 We give thanks to God and the Father of our Lord Jesus Christ, praying always for you,

4 Since we heard of your faith in Christ Jesus, and of the love which ye have to all the saints, 5 For the hope which is laid up for you in heaven, whereof ye heard before in the word of the truth of the gospel;

6 Which is come unto you, as it is in all the world; and bringeth forth fruit, as it doth also in you, since the day ye heard of it, and knew the grace of God in truth:

7 As ye also learned of Epaphras our dear fellow servant, who is for you a faithful minister of Christ;

8 Who also declared unto us your love in the Spirit.

9 For this cause we also, since the day we heard it, do not cease to pray for you, and to desire that ye might be filled with the knowledge of his will in all wisdom and spiritual understanding;

10 That ye might walk worthy of the Lord unto all pleasing, being fruitful in every good work, and increasing in the knowledge of God;

11 Strengthened with all might, according to his glorious power, unto all patience and longsuffering with joyfulness;

12 Giving thanks unto the Father, which hath made us meet to be partakers of the inheritance of the saints in light:

13 Who hath delivered us from the power of darkness, and hath translated us into the kingdom of his dear Son:

14 In whom we have redemption through his blood, even the forgiveness of sins:

Live, move, and have your being in this wonderful mercy, and grace!

Chapter 15

ALL THINGS TO ALL PEOPLE

As a pastor I see people in every stage of life. On a typical Sunday morning I will have people come in the throes of heaviness. Maybe they have lost a loved one, heard devastating news of health issues, a divorce has taken place, and a child has overdosed. These are just some of the issues weekly that as a pastor I must deal with. I have to abide in Jesus to have the compassion He has for them.

At the same time a new baby has been born and the families are rejoicing. Perhaps an engagement has just been announced, a retirement, a move, and so many other circumstances. Philippians 4: 11-13, *"Not that I speak in respect of want: for I have learned, in whatsoever state I am, therewith to be content. I know both how to be abased, and I know how to abound: everywhere and in all things I am instructed both to be full and to be hungry, both to abound and to suffer need. I can do all things through Christ which stengtheneth me."*

As a pastor my prayer life has to be consistent, full of mercy, and compassion. There is no greater love than serving our Savior. It is my prayer that whatever stage of life you are going through that you know He loves you, will never forsake you, and that you will soar with Him.

Being a pastor is probably the most difficult position one could hold and the most rewarding place God could put you in. Many people don't understand the position of leadership God puts a pastor in for you, your family, your community, and the nation.

Some pastors are called to make national social change. Martin Luther King was a pastor with that mantle. As a pastor I speak truth from the Word of God that keeps you out of danger, mistakes, and consequences. It is my pleasure to introduce you to the God of Creation and His Son, Jesus Christ.

As a pastor I believe it is my obligation to set an example of a good marriage, father, and leader. It is my responsibility to motivate you according to Scripture to work, live, and be a part of a godly community. More than anything I have the privilege every Sunday morning to help usher in the presence of the Lord in our services. In His presence there is salvation, healing, joy, life, and love beyond measure.

I know life can be hard and that is one of the reasons I wrote this book. I wanted to give you a parable, story, illustration, that would make it easier for you to understand that life's stuff can be changed by the power of God in your life.

He sees you and hears your cry. He answers and He brings you into an abundant life if you will only let Him take you through the process of His Son's love for you.

As a pastor it is my desire to teach you to become a habitation for the Holy Spirit to dwell in. Let praise and worship fill your body, soul, and spirit. Let yourself be healed. I'll be looking up into the skies and know I will see you soaring one day soon. Stay encouraged!

TO CONTACT:

PASTORS LARRY AND LINDA BISHOP

P.O. BOX 180

JENKS, OK 74037

TELEPHONE

918-296-0077

EMAIL:

info@doveministry.org

doveinc@swbell.net

To Order Books:

booksbydove.com

NOTES

47822635R00098

Made in the USA
Middletown, DE
03 September 2017